ONE
NATION
WITHOUT
LAW

"From Islamic terrorism to the murder of police officers to violent street protests and rampant anti-Semitism, it seems that today's world—and our nation—is on fire. This spirit of lawlessness is increasing in its intensity, and in this powerful and timely new book, Phil Hotsenpiller explains what it all means for America, for the Body of Christ and for the world. Pastor Phil takes us on a fascinating and eye-opening journey through the history of lawlessness, from Genesis to Revelation to today, and shows why followers of Jesus are not to despair in these perilous, uncertain times. Rather, we are to go on the offensive against the lawless wave as a light in the darkness, equipped with the full armor of God and the unassailable truth of the Gospel. *One Nation without Law* is both a prophetic warning and an inspiring call to action. A must-read."

Erick Stakelbeck, host, TBN's *The Watchman*;
director, Christians United for Israel's Watchman Project

"Phil Hotsenpiller has written an important work addressing lawlessness as seen through the ages. From a devout Christian perspective, he analyzes its causes, presenting a Bible-based view of the problem and solution. This book connects current events with a positive look to the future through reliance on faith and prophecy."

Elliot Chodoff, major (reserve), Israel Defense Forces;
director, Strategic Solutions

"Phil's treatment of the presence of lawlessness in our culture is unmatched, but with every detail of apparent negativity, he draws the reader closer toward a counterpoint of hope. This book is a must-read for anyone wanting to better understand this complicated spiritual-political-cultural topic and discover how to race toward the security that is found in our God."

Brock Shinen, Esq., Law Office of Brock Shinen

"In light of society's deteriorating views and lack of adherence to today's laws, Pastor Hotsenpiller offers us both a historical explanation and a cause for supported biblical hope for the future. Here are understanding and answers for changing our today with a stronger spirit and a faith-filled future. An excellent and inspiring read!"

Ward L. Smith, chief of police (retired),
Placentia (California) Police Department

"Clear, concise historical perspective of the real dangers of lawlessness! This truthful account of the existential danger that we face in our War on Terror across the globe brings to life God's law in the Old Testament and His 'blueprint' for life—and how to combat lawlessness in our everyday lives. A remarkable piece of work!"

Michael P. Chené, colonel (retired),
United States Marine Corps

ONE NATION WITHOUT LAW

THE RISE OF LAWLESSNESS, THE END TIMES
AND THE POWER OF HOPE

PHIL HOTSENPILLER

Chosen

a division of Baker Publishing Group
Minneapolis, Minnesota

© 2017 by Phillip Hotsenpiller

Published by Chosen Books
11400 Hampshire Avenue South
Bloomington, Minnesota 55438
www.chosenbooks.com

Chosen Books is a division of
Baker Publishing Group, Grand Rapids, Michigan

Printed in the United States of America

Library of Congress Control Number: 2017000007.

ISBN 978-0-8007-9843-7

Cover design by Rob Williams, InsideOutCreativeArts

Author is represented by The FEDD Agency, Inc.

17 18 19 20 21 22 23   7 6 5 4 3 2 1

I dedicate this book to Tammy, my wife, my friend, mother of our children and colleague in ministry. Your devotion to God and His Kingdom is a daily inspiration to me. I love you and look forward to all that God has planned for us in the future.

Contents

Foreword

PHIL HOTSENPILLER HAS ACCOMPLISHED something rare in his new book, *One Nation without Law*. He shares a theological and hope-filled perspective on how to position our faith while trying to understand lawlessness and evil in the world around us. Theologically, we have lived in the dark ages regarding these subjects, but through the power of Phil's own personal experiences as well as his historical interpretation of both modern and ancient history, you will find yourself on an empowered journey.

I remember when I was wrapped up in one of the worst seasons of being affected by lawlessness I have ever experienced. Our house was broken into, some people working for us had been lying to us and slandering us, I had to deal with an identity-theft situation and some of our teams in foreign nations were robbed. It was a brutal perfect storm of corruption around us, and I began to ask all the hard questions: *Why are people so evil? When will God vindicate us? Why did this happen to me when I am trying to follow God?*

During that time I had to come to a place of conviction based on my biblical beliefs in the nature of God. I wish I had also had this book, because when you don't have understanding, your choices to live in hope and strength of conviction are not as clear. I came to a great place, but it probably took me way longer than it needed to.

I believe many good Christians live in spiritual confusion about who God is in the midst of lawlessness. What is God's role when we are experiencing suffering at the hands of corruption or even evil? How do we evaluate our choices, and even how do we keep an open heart to hope in these times? How do we pray or look to God, and how do we position our faith? Why are there lawless people on the earth? Thank God for Phil, who expertly answers these questions and raises the bar in creating an easily accessible clarity over God's very nature in the midst of humanity's weakness and sin.

Phil's role as part historian, part theologian and all pastor will help ground you in a winning world and Bible-based view. You will be blessed, and you will grow from your time with this book. It is time for this biblical perspective to empower us so that we don't give the wrong message about who God is, instead focusing on how beautiful a life in God can be in the midst of a world filled with lawlessness.

Shawn Bolz, bestselling author, *Translating God*
and *Keys to Heaven's Economy*;
TV host and Los Angeles–based pastor,
www.BolzMinistries.com

Introduction

A PRODUCER FOR THE HISTORY CHANNEL asked me to participate in a program on the end of the world, featuring specialists whose expertise ranged from Bible prophecy to quantum physics. The producer and his film crew were genuinely interested in exploring the mystery of the future. After I had fielded questions for more than three hours, he approached me, off camera, and asked, "Phil, when you think about the future, what scares you?"

Without hesitation I responded, "Lawlessness."

I am not sure what he expected my answer to be, but the shock on his face was evident. I went on to explain that my greatest fear about the future is when lawlessness becomes—and it is now becoming—a normal part of mainstream culture.

It is difficult to watch the news these days without some degree of frustration, fear and trepidation. The daily reports of lawless actions in the societies we live in appear not only more widespread but also more intense than ever.

Is nowhere safe? We have experienced terror—from without and within—in our schools, in our workplaces, in our theaters, at major sporting events and in our skies. Even churches are not immune to the pervasive lawlessness that has so thoroughly infected the prevailing culture. If this is a prophetic spread of lawlessness—and it certainly appears to be—it is likely to get worse before it gets better.

How, then, are we to respond to such mounting lawlessness? Wring our hands? Panic? Run for the hills? Join the high-volume rhetoric on radio call-in shows?

A far better option for confronting our fears and frustrations is to learn to see the issue from God's perspective. In the chapters that follow, we will find that the problem is by no means a new one. God is well aware of what is taking place in the world (as He always has been), and He has a plan to restore perfect peace to His people. In the meantime, we will pull back the curtain and peer behind the rampant lawlessness surrounding us, and we will consider some appropriate ways to respond.

To start, we will take a look at the rise of lawlessness, tracing its roots and its spread through the centuries. Our examination will involve both history and geography, uncovering the influence of lawlessness in various places and how its influence is now making inroads even in the United States.

From there we will examine a variety of prophecies about lawlessness and its connection to the end times. We will consider how the timing of certain current world events makes some such prophecies especially relevant. They point to an even greater escalation of lawlessness on a worldwide scale. Seen from a human perspective, things may appear bleak indeed. But as we consider the spiritual perspective of those same events, we will see what purpose these struggles serve in God's plan.

Finally, we want to explore options we can take to respond appropriately to the rising tide of lawlessness around us. When we begin to see God's perspective on such events, we are better equipped to put our fears and anxieties into His capable hands and move on with our lives. As we renew the invitation He has made for us to put our hope in Him, we become more empowered to take a stand when we need to and not be so quick either to cower or clumsily rampage against the injustices we see. We continue to grow spiritually stronger, even in the lengthening shadows of lawlessness and evil.

Regardless of what we see on the news, God is still in control. His control is not limited to any region or country; He is the Lord, and He directs the paths of all mankind. And we can move forward with hopeful determination to make our world a better place.

THE RISE OF LAWLESSNESS

EVERY GENERATION SEEMS to imagine that the next one is shaping up to be worse: more self-centered, less spiritually aware, morally weaker and so forth. But lately the statistics are beginning to bear out the truth that our world is in a definite slide deeper and deeper into lawlessness. This section will define *lawlessness* as I am using the term and will lay out the increasing severity of the problem, both in the United States and worldwide. The disturbing truth, as we will see, is that the spirit of lawlessness may be both more prevalent and more personal than we might have considered.

1

The Problem of Lawlessness

THE PEOPLE QUAKED in their sandals. Above them, the mountaintop was shrouded in a thick cloud, bringing thunder and lightning much too close for comfort. Simultaneously, the mountain began to spew impenetrable smoke and tremble violently. A trumpet reverberated from the heavens, growing louder and louder.

At the mountain's foot, the terrified people struggled to take in everything that was happening around them. They had been warned not to set foot on the mountain under penalty of death. Not a problem! But Moses was fearless, speaking in the midst of the turmoil, and the people heard God's voice in response.

It is not like they had not already witnessed miracles, one after another. Only weeks ago they had been slaves to one of the mightiest empires on earth—the Egyptians. Then this man Moses had appeared, promising that God would soon free them. Of course the Egyptians had resisted, and the Israelites saw judgment fall on their captors in the form of plagues as God persistently goaded Pharaoh to release the people.

Even after Pharaoh finally relented, he changed his mind and unleashed his army to retrieve his former slaves. God orchestrated their escape by parting the Red Sea, sending the Israelites through on dry land with walls of standing water on either side (and drowning the pursuing army in the process). God fed them in a barren land with bread from heaven and provided water in miraculous ways—one time out of solid rock! God's presence stood constantly before them in a pillar of cloud by day and pillar of fire by night.

It was enough to keep the adrenaline surging. But this . . . their extended stay at Mount Sinai . . . this was something beyond anything they had seen or imagined. What could possibly warrant such a solemn and portentous occasion?[1]

God called Moses to ascend the mountain into the cloud, the smoke, the thunder and the lightning for one purpose: to receive the Law. God had agreed to be the Israelites' God and protector, and through the Law He was letting them know what He expected of them in exchange. He would soon take them to the land He had promised Abraham and his descendants, and He was preparing them for a lifestyle quite different from that of the surrounding peoples.

Other nations had already created codes of law, so a new code was not especially significant. What was absolutely unprecedented on this day was God's reaching down to make a holy covenant with His people, through which He would codify His promises and expectations. Though most people at this time would have been familiar with a single individual as king or leader, they were unable to comprehend a single god who was sovereign over *everything*. The Egyptians, for example, acknowledged hundreds of gods connected with the sun, the sky, the earth, the dead, the desert and most aspects of life. In contrast, monotheism was a new concept that would stand against the beliefs of (and be challenged by) almost every other culture the Israelites would encounter.

For the thousands of people trembling at the foot of Mount Sinai, it could not have been more evident that their God was the author of their Law, and it was to be taken seriously.

What Is "Lawlessness"?

Why am I starting this book with a history lesson? Because before we can begin to comprehend the mystery of lawlessness, we need to try to understand the extraordinary imparting of the Law. Most Christian denominations naturally tend to emphasize New Testament doctrines like grace and mercy over the Law, yet a fundamental understanding of the Law is what makes such tenets so meaningful.

Jewish communities of faith, on the other hand, are frequently noted for their devotion to the Torah, the first five books of the Bible. At the time of this writing, a *USA Today* story is reporting about a rabbi in New Brunswick, New Jersey, who, in spite of his synagogue being engulfed in fire, ran inside to retrieve a cherished Torah. As he ran out with it, the ceiling collapsed behind him.[2]

Yet the real significance of the Law is not so much whether it is handwritten on a parchment scroll or typeset in a favorite Bible as much as whether it is written on one's heart and mind. The Law represents a relationship with the Lawgiver. From time to time in Judeo-Christian history, its significance has waned and even essentially disappeared. Yet we would do well to remember that God initiated this covenant with humankind and gave us the Law, not as a series of hoops to jump through to please Him but as a blueprint for life so that we maximize our relationships with Him and with one another. Those who genuinely love God will automatically want to do what He says, strengthening their relationships with Him because they know He has their best interests at heart.

Some people innately resist being told what to do by anyone, including God (or, perhaps, especially by God). This is the essence of lawlessness. When we are aware of the holy solemnity that went into God's giving of the Law, we see what a terrible offense such defiance is to God.

When I speak of lawlessness, I am not talking about well-intentioned believers or seekers who are trying to be good disciples yet stumble occasionally (or even frequently) along the way. That is a part of everyone's personal spiritual growth. But lawlessness is intentional. It is an awareness that God has set specific parameters for our actions—whether we bother to determine what they are or not—and a callous disregard of His Law in order to follow our own desires and passions.

In fact, lawlessness existed long before the Law did, predating even human history. Adam and Eve had hardly set up house in the Garden of Eden before the serpent came along and led them to question God's precise instructions—and, more importantly, His motives (see Genesis 3:1–5). The consequences of their defiant actions were expulsion from the garden, a life made much more challenging and a subsequent awkward distance in the relationship between God and humans.

A few centuries later, Moses had not even made it down from Mount Sinai with the completed Law before the Israelites had given up on him and formed a golden calf to be their god. (Their fear of God, though real, was apparently very short lived.) The resulting consequences were not pretty. Even after Moses interceded for the people to prevent God from destroying them, many of them paid for their lawless, thoughtless behavior (Exodus 32:9–14, 25–28, 35).

God finally got His people to the Promised Land, but they went whining most of the way and ended up taking a forty-year "time out" before arriving. We will look at more recent and even more offensive examples of lawlessness in later chapters.

Civil Law

Despite the significance of the Law in Judeo-Christian history, when most of us hear the word *law*, we do not think of Moses. Most likely we think of the local, state and national rules that govern society. It has long been understood that when people cluster together to form communities, cities or nations, they need a clear set of laws that all are expected to follow.

One of the best-known early sets of laws was the Code of Hammurabi, which dates back to the mid-1700s BC. Hammurabi was a Babylonian king who ruled more than forty years. His code contained 282 laws grouped logically (contract law, buying and selling, guidelines for relationships, etc.) and written so everyone could understand clearly what was expected. In essence, it served as an early constitution for Hammurabi's culture. An archaeologist discovered the code in 1901, inscribed in cuneiform script on a seven-and-a-half-foot stele shaped like an index finger. You can see it in the Louvre.

Wise leaders have since discovered that Hammurabi was on to something. When overseeing a group of people, large or small, it is easier to establish up front what rules will guide their behavior and interactions.

This was the pattern followed by leaders of the American colonies when it came time to establish the colonies as a nation. First, they composed a Declaration of Independence, explaining in detail why they were breaking ties with Great Britain. One of their first stated grievances was that the English king "has refused his Assent to Laws, the most wholesome and necessary for the public good."

The Colonial leaders followed up this bold declaration with a detailed Constitution, spelling out the rules of government and the rights of citizenship. It is no coincidence that, as you will see if you study the historical records, the founding fathers were steadfastly devoted to the biblical laws that Moses received thousands of years earlier.

With the guidance of the Declaration of Independence and legal umbrella of the Constitution in place, numerous state and local laws have been established to oversee and guide the citizens of our nation. Americans tend to complain about the "red tape," "loopholes" and such in the sheer number of laws and vast complexity of our legal system, but we should be thankful we have it. The law may be confusing at times, but it provides security. A lawless society (or world) is a scary one. When even a few people ignore the law of the land or treat it with contempt, it creates danger for everyone.

To give an example, we pass laws requiring drivers to stop at red lights. Most of us have an innate sense of the right thing to do, whether or not we choose to do it; but it is not good enough that 95 percent of drivers agree that it is the right thing to do and do so voluntarily. The other 5 percent would still do tremendous damage to themselves and others if allowed to disregard the restriction. To prevent this, citations are handed out for running a red light. The stakes are higher, of course, for more serious matters: robbery, assault, sexual offenses, murder and so on. Even when laws are established and enforced, intentional affronts to the law create tremendous problems for society as a whole.

Throughout this book I will use the term *lawlessness* to refer not to minor infractions or small segments of society that break the law. Rather, I will use a much broader sense of the term to indicate a time when the rule of law is no longer acknowledged as the basis for society.

If you get a speeding ticket, you have broken the law. Technically, that might make you a lawless person, but that is not the lawlessness I am speaking of. You may have been unintentionally careless, which is true of most of us at times. Perhaps your genuine concern about some emergency at home caused you to subliminally press your foot on the accelerator a bit too hard in your haste.

If you saw the 55 mph sign, however, and then went barreling down the interstate at 80 mph because you just did not care what the authorities thought, or you thought it should be your right to drive as fast as you want to, then you might have the seeds of a lawless attitude that could become problematic if it carries over to other matters. It is this purposeful and intensifying flouting of the law on a wide-scale basis that will be the topic of this book.

What Mystery?

Occasionally I refer to "the *mystery* of lawlessness." I do not think many of us would question the *presence* of lawlessness these days, but I intend to delve deeper by addressing the source, the anticipation of and the predicted future for lawlessness. As such, it is indeed a mystery, though still not in the sense that most of us use the word.

We may think of a mystery as something for Sherlock Holmes to solve after he accumulates sufficient clues and puts the facts together in just the right manner. The biblical concept of mystery, however, does not quite fit that definition. Nor does it refer to weighty, secret information that only a devoted few can discern (this was the alluring promise of certain first-century sects developing at about the same time as Christianity).

A biblical mystery is a truth that is understood only after it is revealed by God. It remains unseen by the unenlightened but is clearly evident to those who have spiritual insight—those of whom Jesus frequently said, "He who has ears to hear, let him hear!" (Matthew 11:15; 13:9, 43; and many others). Multitudes could hear the same teaching from Jesus' mouth, and some would take home deep spiritual truths while others missed the point altogether. A biblical mystery can either reveal truth or conceal truth—or both, as in 1 Corinthians 2:7–8. The apostle Paul referred to the Gospel itself as a mystery (see Colossians 1:24–27).

Biblical mysteries are outside the range of natural comprehension (see 1 Corinthians 2:13–16). Regardless of intelligence, experiences or desire, we are incapable of comprehending the things of God until His Spirit enlightens us. Paul refers back to Isaiah 64:4 when he reminds us,

> As it is written: "Eye has not seen, nor ear heard, nor have entered into the heart of man the things which God has prepared for those who love Him." But God has revealed them to us through His Spirit. For the Spirit searches all things, yes, the deep things of God.
>
> 1 Corinthians 2:9–10

Because God's mysteries are understandable only through divine revelation, it can be surprising who "gets it" and who does not. In the first century, many of the Jewish Pharisees and Sadducees were as educated in the things of God as anyone could be. They thought they had a good handle on the Law and the prophets and how the teachings of Scripture should be applied to everyday life. Yet Jesus was regularly at odds with them, even as they were befuddled by His teachings and miracles. He saw clearly their hypocrisy and called them on it, yet they were unable to see that He was clearly fulfilling the plan of God. They just could not figure out the mystery. As Jesus called people to come to Him and, in doing so, get closer to God the Father, He prayed, "I thank You, Father, Lord of heaven and earth, that You have hidden these things from the wise and prudent and have revealed them to babes" (Matthew 11:25).

One more point about biblical mysteries: God reveals them at His appointed time. When Jesus began to teach using parables, His disciples asked Him why. Among other things, He told them,

> Because it has been given to you to know the mysteries of the kingdom of heaven, but to them it has not been given. . . . But blessed are your eyes for they see, and your ears for they hear; for assuredly, I say to you that many prophets and righteous men desired to see what you see, and did not see it, and to hear what you hear, and did not hear it.
>
> Matthew 13:11, 16–17

At one point during the era of the biblical kings, the king of Israel was at war with the king of Syria. God gave Elisha the prophet remarkable insight into everything Syria planned, allowing him to warn the king of Israel and avoid serious trouble. Elisha's fore-warnings were so accurate that before long the king of Syria thought he had a traitor in his midst; at the urging of his officers he determined to capture Elisha and bring him in, sending an impressive military force to encircle him.

Elisha's servant looked out the next morning and saw a multitude of Syrian horses and chariots. He was naturally fearful. But Elisha immediately assured him, "Those who are with us are more than those who are with them" (2 Kings 6:16). He then prayed, "Lord . . . open his eyes that he may see" (verse 17). When the servant looked out again, he no longer noticed the Syrian forces but instead saw the area dense with horses and chariots *of fire*—God's forces.

The presence and power of God had been there all along, but the servant could not see it until God revealed it to him. But what a difference it made in his outlook on life! It is my prayer that, as we undergo this examination of lawlessness, God will open your eyes and ears so that truth is revealed and you arrive at a much better understanding that will improve your perspective.

It Comes as No Surprise

God is neither shocked nor taken by surprise by the lawlessness He sees among humankind. Indeed, Jesus told us to expect it. He looked down the corridors of time, far beyond His own impending death and resurrection, and He told His disciples what to expect. Among numerous teachings about the end of the age, He told them,

> Many will be offended, will betray one another, and will hate one another. Then many false prophets will rise up and deceive many. And because lawlessness will abound, the love of many will grow cold. But he who endures to the end shall be saved. And this gospel of the kingdom will be preached in all the world as a witness to all the nations, and then the end will come.
>
> Matthew 24:10–14

The apostle Paul would soon confirm what Jesus was teaching. He, too, was aware of a grim time in the world's future when lawlessness would increase to unprecedented heights. He warned of a powerful and horrible "man of lawlessness" one day arising; in the meantime,

> the mystery of lawlessness is already at work; only He who now restrains will do so until He is taken out of the way. And then the lawless one will be revealed, whom the Lord will consume with the breath of His mouth and destroy with the brightness of His coming.
>
> 2 Thessalonians 2:7–8

Thus the "mystery of lawlessness" was already beginning to spread in the first century and continues to gain momentum; yet it is still being restrained by God. Lawlessness is progressive and will someday reach its full power when God removes His restraint. Is that day coming soon? That is part of the mystery we will explore. In later chapters we will examine these and other prophecies in much more detail. But for now let's not miss one key point to keep in mind as we go through this book. Without a doubt, biblical descriptions of things to come and events of the end times can create a sense of worry and foreboding. Sometimes they are taken out of context and used as scare tactics. But as you approach these wonderful and enlightening passages, never forget that they were provided for the *encouragement* of the faithful.

Take another look at Jesus' warning about the last days in Matthew 24. For some people, all that will register will be what He says about betrayal, hatred, deceit and lawlessness. While Jesus did indeed give us fair warning about these, He also spoke of endurance . . . of salvation . . . of the spread of the Gospel. He indicated that we have some choices as to how we will respond to the awful things we witness in our world.

October 2, 2006, began as a gorgeous Indian summer morning in Lancaster County, Pennsylvania. In the small Amish community of Nickel Mines, the children went as usual to their one-room schoolhouse. Meanwhile, a non-Amish, 32-year-old milk truck driver named Charlie Roberts got home from his shift, walked his children to catch the bus to their own school and kissed them good-bye. Shortly afterward he drove to the Amish school and, brandishing weapons, ordered the adults and all the boys to leave. He then tied the hands and feet of ten girls between the ages of six and thirteen and had them lie down facing the blackboard. Police arrived and tried to talk Roberts into surrendering, but he continued to threaten violence and eventually began shooting each victim in the back of the head, before shooting himself.

Two girls died at the schoolhouse, as did Roberts. Another young girl was pronounced dead by the time she got to the nearest hospital, and two others were removed from life support and died the following morning. All the surviving girls were hospitalized with varying degrees of injury. One victim was left with serious brain injuries, unable to walk or talk. Speculation for Roberts's motive was that nine years previously a daughter of his own had died only twenty minutes after being born. He had agonized over her death and expressed anger toward God at times.

The incident received national attention, of course, but what followed really ensured that this day would not be quickly forgotten. The shooting took place at about 11:00 a.m., yet that very afternoon the Amish community, including close relatives of the victims, turned out to comfort Roberts's widow, parents and in-laws. Donald Kraybill, a local sociologist, said, "Several families, Amish families who had buried their own daughters just the day before were in attendance [at Roberts's burial service at the cemetery] and they hugged the widow, and hugged other members of the killer's family."[3] It was reported that there were more Amish than non-Amish at Roberts's funeral.

Even now that a decade has passed, certain scars remain from that terrible day. Victims continue to deal with physical challenges. The boys who escaped the tragedy have undergone survivors' guilt. Families still miss their loved ones. But the very next week after the shooting took place, a group of Amish men demolished the schoolhouse, leaving in its place a pasture. They rebuilt the school—renamed the New Hope School—and it opened six months after the incident. Although they could not undo all the damage that had taken place, they did what they could to remove the dark stain of lawlessness from their community.

Most of us will never expect to even approach the degree of forgiveness, grace and mercy offered by the Amish community in the wake of this almost indescribable act of lawlessness. We need to see, however, that evil need not have the last word. We do not *have* to respond to terror around us with a knee-jerk reaction of cowering, flailing out in rage or plotting revenge. We do have options as to how we respond to lawlessness. We can make more of an effort to heed the rest of Jesus' warning about lawlessness—the part about endurance, salvation and the spread of the Gospel. Even if we have not yet reached the spiritual level to respond as we might wish, we should see that it is indeed possible.

As you read on from here, ask God to open your eyes and ears to reveal things you have never understood before. I pray that this book will be a helpful resource for you, yet it is not likely to do you much good unless you trust the Spirit of God to guide you to His truth. As we turn our attention to the evil all around, keep in mind that it is the same Spirit who can provide all you need to respond more effectively when the world around you is falling apart.

2

The Evil in All of Us

ADOLF EICHMANN, member of the SS, rose from the rank of file clerk to become one of the most notorious figures of Nazi Germany. A recognized "Jewish specialist" within the SS, he collected information on prominent Jews, amassed pages of notes from his visits to various Jewish communities and participated in Jewish meetings. He even studied Hebrew.

When the Nazis began to consider potential "solutions to the Jewish question," Eichmann was a logical choice to plan and advise. His first step was to establish a Central Office for Jewish Emigration in Vienna in 1938. Using his organizational and business acumen, he set up an "assembly line" through which "a Jew could [show] up at the Central Emigration Office with his papers and proceed from desk to desk until he arrived at the end, with a passport and an exit visa but stripped of his property, cash and rights."[1] Almost a hundred thousand Austrian Jews ceded their wealth to Eichmann's office in order to leave the country—a system so profitable that similar offices were soon established in other German-controlled cities.[2]

The next year Eichmann moved to Berlin to oversee a Gestapo office responsible for establishing policies and procedures for Nazi interaction with Jews. He continued to promote emigration as a means of ridding the German Reich of Jews; by early 1942, however, this had become unfeasible, and Nazi leadership decided to invest their resources in the systematic murder of Jews within their controlled territories. Eichmann became the logistical chief of this operation, given the responsibility of forcing the evacuation of and deporting millions of Jews, first into ghettos and later to the death camps.

He performed his duties with zeal, lending his tacit approval as Jews were sent to camps and stripped of everything of value. Healthy individuals were subjected to forced labor, while their young children and older relatives were exterminated. In 1944, Eichmann personally oversaw the deportation of more than 400,000 Hungarian Jews in eight weeks, most of whom were murdered on arrival in the infamous Auschwitz concentration camp. He was reported by fellow Nazis to have said that he would "leap laughing into the grave because the feeling that he had five million enemies of the Reich on his conscience would be for him a source of extraordinary satisfaction."[3]

Eichmann was arrested after the war and placed in an American internment camp. He escaped and fled to Argentina but was located by Israeli Mossad agents in 1960, tried in Jerusalem and found guilty on all counts. He was sentenced to death and hanged in 1962.[4]

Among those testifying against Eichmann at his trial was a Polish Jew named Yehiel Dinur, who had survived two years in Auschwitz. In the middle of his testimony, Dinur underwent a physical and emotional breakdown. In a *60 Minutes* interview 22 years later, Mike Wallace showed Dinur a film clip of him sobbing and then collapsing and asked, "What happened to you at that moment?"

Wallace might have expected a wide range of answers—fear, anger, bitterness, regret, haunting memories, sorrow or rage. Dinur's answer surprised him: "I was afraid about myself. I saw that I am capable to do this . . . exactly like he." Dinur had realized in that moment that Eichmann was just an ordinary man who had succumbed to the sin and evil that we all struggle with as human beings.

Wallace asked how it was possible for any man to do the things Eichmann did. "Was he a monster? A madman? Or was he perhaps something even more terrifying . . . was he normal?"

Yehiel Dinur had no doubt. He simply stated, "Eichmann is in all of us."[5]

Why does evil exist? Philosophers have debated the question for centuries, while the rest of us struggle to make sense of horrific actions that we witness—actions that seem to come more and more frequently. We compare ourselves to others and reason, *I'm not as bad as this person or that group.* Yet inwardly we realize that we are part of the problem. There is no denying it: All of us are deeply, tragically flawed.

Why can we not just do what is right? Because evil dwells in all of us. In order to resolve the problem, we need the courage to see ourselves correctly. Only then can we develop the necessary blend of humility and boldness—first to change our own way of thinking and then to fight against evil in our world. The ability to change, though, is not a result of personal guilt or self-condemnation; change comes only by experiencing God's love, grace and acceptance.

An Old, Old Problem

The problem of lawlessness and evil is by no means new. We get no further than the second verse of Scripture to discover that something seems to be amiss.

The familiar opening statement of the Bible shows us that "in the beginning God created the heavens and the earth" (Genesis 1:1). Elsewhere we are told clearly that God "did not create it [the earth] in vain, who formed it to be inhabited" (Isaiah 45:18).

Yet by the time we get to the second verse of Genesis 1, we discover that the earth *was* "without form, and void" and "darkness was on the face of the deep." In addition, we see light contending with darkness in verses 3–4. It stands to reason that this is a spiritual contention because the physical sources of light (sun, moon, stars) were not created until the fourth day (verses 14–19). What happened between verse 1 and verse 2 that caused God's perfect world to become dark and empty?

A number of clues were revealed to the prophets and are embedded in Scripture to help us look behind the scenes, even before human time began. First, let's examine a passage from Isaiah:

How you are fallen from heaven, O Lucifer, son of the morning! How you are cut down to the ground, you who weakened the nations! For you have said in your heart: "I will ascend into heaven, I will exalt my throne above the stars of God; I will also sit on the mount of the congregation on the farthest sides of the north; I will ascend above the heights of the clouds, I will be like the Most High." Yet you shall be brought down to Sheol, to the lowest depths of the Pit.

Isaiah 14:12–15

Your Bible translation may not refer to Lucifer by name; many simply identify him as "daystar," "morning star" or some similar description. Yet it seems evident that this is the figure who is eventually known as the deceiver . . . the devil . . . Satan.

I believe Lucifer was created in splendor and perfection on a level with angels such as Michael, Gabriel and others in the upper echelon of God's heavenly host. We know that through Christ God created all things "that are in heaven and that are on earth, visible and invisible, whether thrones or dominions or principalities or powers" (Colossians 1:16). Lucifer was certainly no exception.

Yet we see in Isaiah 14 that Lucifer rebelled against God. His desire to rise above the "stars" of God is probably a reference to other angels. (See Revelation 1:20 for another example of angels being referred to as "stars.") His ultimate goal, however, was to rise to the level of God Himself. His intent to ascend into heaven suggests that he was on earth at the time. It was an attempted power grab that failed miserably, as we see also in Ezekiel:

> Moreover the word of the LORD came to me, saying, "Son of man, take up a lamentation for the king of Tyre, and say to him, 'Thus says the Lord GOD: You were the seal of perfection, full of wisdom and perfect in beauty. You were in Eden, the garden of God; every precious stone was your covering: the sardius, topaz, and diamond, beryl, onyx, and jasper, sapphire, turquoise, and emerald with gold. The workmanship of your timbrels and pipes was prepared for you on the day you were created.
>
> "'You were the anointed cherub who covers; I established you; you were on the holy mountain of God; you walked back and forth in the midst of fiery stones. You were perfect in your ways from the day you were created, till iniquity was found in you.
>
> "'By the abundance of your trading you became filled with violence within, and you sinned; therefore I cast you as a profane thing out of the mountain of God; and I destroyed you, O covering cherub, from the midst of the fiery stones.
>
> "'Your heart was lifted up because of your beauty; you corrupted your wisdom for the sake of your splendor; I cast you to the ground, I laid you before kings, that they might gaze at you.
>
> "'You defiled your sanctuaries by the multitude of your iniquities, by the iniquity of your trading; therefore I brought fire from

your midst; it devoured you, and I turned you to ashes upon the earth in the sight of all who saw you. All who knew you among the peoples are astonished at you; you have become a horror, and shall be no more forever.'"

Ezekiel 28:11–19

Though this passage at first glance appears to be a continuation of the judgment against the "prince of Tyre" (verse 2), it could not possibly be speaking of the same person:

> In 28:1–10 Ezekiel rebuked the *ruler* [Hebrew *nagiyd*] for claiming to be a god though he was just a man. But in verses 11–19 Ezekiel described the *king* [Hebrew *melek*] in terms that could not apply to a mere man. This "king" had appeared in the Garden of Eden (verse 13), had been a guardian cherub (verse 14a), had possessed free access to God's holy mountain (verse 14b), and had been sinless from the time he was created (verse 15).[6]

I believe this figure is Lucifer, and that Ezekiel is giving us a parallel account to Isaiah's. At the beginning Ezekiel describes a magnificent, sinless being who had not yet led a rebellion against God. By Genesis 3, Lucifer had begun to manifest wickedness, violence and sin; as a result he lost his privileges in Eden and was "cast out," replaced by Adam as God's designated overseer of the Garden (see Genesis 2:15).

I believe the spiritual attack on Adam by Lucifer in Genesis 3 was based on the principle of dominion. Lucifer's dominion in Eden had been given over to Adam, so Lucifer sought to get even by drawing Adam away from God, resulting in Adam's loss of dominion over Eden—and worse.

By Genesis 10 we see lawlessness beginning to coalesce into a kingdom with a human leader named Nimrod, who is linked with the formation of Babel (later Babylon; see Genesis 10:8–12). The first thing we learn about Babel is its inhabitants' defiance of God's instructions to fill the earth after the flood (see Genesis 9:1). The people of Babel had other plans: "Come, let us build ourselves a city, and a tower whose top is in the heavens; let us make a name for ourselves, lest we be scattered abroad over the face of the whole earth" (Genesis 11:4). As happens to anyone who opposes God, their plans were thwarted.

From its origin, Babel was the antithesis of what God desired. In time, Babylon became more than a physical, earthly kingdom; it was actually an evil religious system woven throughout history that perpetually attracted sinful humankind to it.

Nimrod also established Nineveh, the eventual capital of Assyria. The Babylonians and Assyrians would become two of the ancient world's mightiest forces, creating havoc for God's people for centuries.

Lawlessness and Evil

Lawlessness and evil are not the same thing. Certainly people might occasionally break the law for any number of reasons: desperation, ignorance, panic (running red lights to get a pregnant wife to the hospital to deliver the baby), civil disobedience as protest of unjust laws and so forth. These instances, though unlawful, are not necessarily evil.

Consider the protagonist of Victor Hugo's *Les Misérables*, Jean Valjean, who struggled to live with a criminal record that began when he was sentenced to five years in prison for stealing a loaf of bread to feed his sister's seven starving children. His was a lawless act, to be sure, but there was no evil intent behind it. Yet after four escape attempts, Valjean ended up spending nineteen years in jail, and upon release he continued to steal to support himself. As a result, police inspector Javert pursued Valjean relentlessly . . . until Valjean could have killed him but spared his life. Victor Hugo, then, seems to suggest that lawlessness does not always lead to evil.

They are often, however, very closely connected. What happens all too frequently is that lawlessness becomes intentional and repeated. Perhaps someone steals something out of desperation and does not get caught. It becomes easier to steal again . . . and again. Once the line is crossed, for whatever reason, some people find it hard to stop. Lawlessness becomes a way of life—and a threshold that allows all-out evil to reign.

That seems to have been the case with Adolf Eichmann. An argument can be made that he was not born the evil mastermind that history portrays him to be. He was skilled in administration and planning, not violence, and he originally endorsed a plan to relocate all European Jews to Madagascar—a solution that would satisfy his bosses without the brutality of the concentration camps. (The plan was shelved when the war did not end quickly, as expected, and Hitler and the Nazi leadership ordered that the Jews be killed instead.)

Rather than challenge his orders, Eichmann readily set to the task of establishing death camps and ensuring that trains ran consistently to deliver their human cargo for annihilation. At his trial, Eichmann's defense was that he had merely followed orders, to no avail. The Nazi disregard for moral law had intensified into a callous acceptance and willing endorsement of evil. This fact was what startled Dinur so much—few if any of us are immune to such a gradually increasing tolerance of evil.

Throughout this book, when I speak of *lawlessness*, I am referring to a developed spirit of defiance that derives from Satan himself (not occasional actions that derive from bad behavior). That spirit of lawlessness began prior to human creation and the Garden of Eden (Genesis 2–3) and quickly infected God's creation

39

as humankind chose to rebel against Him. It had become manifest in a national way by Genesis 10, and it continues to stand in constant opposition to God and His people. Eventually it will reach its fullest expression under "the man of lawlessness" (see 2 Thessalonians 2)—the Antichrist—until God finally terminates the spirit of lawlessness (Revelation 18).

The increasing influence of the spirit of lawlessness and rise of evil leads to a couple of logical questions: (1) Why did God tolerate the origin of evil to begin with? (2) With things as bad as they currently are, why does God not go ahead and do away with evil . . . *now*? Let's think through these common questions.

Why Did God Tolerate Evil?

The existence of suffering and evil has created great consternation among people in their relationships with God, keeping both theologians and agnostics busy with various accusations and defenses. It is the crux of the book of Job, as the afflicted and despondent father cries out for answers but is left with only more questions.

The Greek philosopher Epicurus was among the first to state clearly what many of us sense instinctively. His "riddle" dates back more than three hundred years before Christ and goes something like this:

Is God willing to prevent evil, but not able? Then he is not omnipotent.

Is he able, but not willing? Then he is malevolent.

Is he both able and willing? Then whence cometh evil?

Is he neither able nor willing? Then why call him God?

At the time, Epicurus was most likely referring to *his* primary deity, Zeus. But the same questions have been asked of the

Judeo-Christian God. At first reading, Epicurus' argument seems to cast our God in a negative light. Skeptics and scoffers callously insist that the existence of evil means that God cannot possibly be both all-powerful and all-loving. But there are holes in such logic.

In his book *The Problem of Pain*, C. S. Lewis offers three reasons why God might indeed permit evil; they are succinctly summarized by Art Lindsley, a senior fellow at the C. S. Lewis Institute.[7] The first is *free will*. God did not create evil, but in giving us the opportunity to choose to love Him, He also leaves open the possibility that we might choose evil instead. As parents, do we want our children to love and obey us only because they have no other choice? Of course not! If God had created us without the opportunity to *choose* to love Him, would that be the best possible world? Lewis acknowledges, "That we used our free wills to become very bad is so well known that it hardly needs to be stated."[8] Still, God grants us that freedom, and as a consequence, evil sometimes is the result.

A second reason is *natural law*. Things that God has created and deemed "good" can still be used for evil purposes by someone with a lawless spirit, and God does not remove their harmful properties when misused. A wooden beam can be used to build a home or wielded as a murder weapon. Sound waves carry lies and insults just as they do praise and worship. The same natural forces (fire, water, sexuality and so forth) that create pleasure can also create physical and/or emotional pain.

Lewis's third reason why God might allow the existence of evil is what he referred to as "soul making," borrowing a phrase from John Keats. For centuries certain people had referred to this earthly life with its pains and tribulations as a "vale of tears." Keats, in a letter to family members, said that he felt those troubles of life (and he certainly had his share) actually constituted a "vale of Soul-making."[9] When confronted with trials and disappointments, we have a choice whether to buckle under them or rise to the challenge of overcoming them. When we choose to persevere, we grow stronger and more spiritually mature.

Lewis agreed:

> I have seen great beauty of spirit in some who were great sufferers. I have seen men, for the most part, grow better not worse with advancing years, and I have seen the last illness produce treasures of fortitude and meekness from most unpromising subjects. I see in loved and revered historical figures . . . traits which might scarcely have been tolerable if the men had been happier. If the world is indeed a "vale of soul-making," it seems on the whole to be doing its work.[10]

Ongoing studies in developmental psychology confirm as much. In going through the stages of life, what propels us from one level to the next are the challenges we face that prod us out of our comfort zones and force us to see the world through a different lens.[11]

Also echoing the thoughts of C. S. Lewis are the findings of contemporary philosopher Alvin Plantinga. Since the 1960s, in talks and books he has proposed a "free will defense" to demonstrate that the presence of evil is not inconsistent with the existence of an omnipotent, omniscient, good God. When we confront evil, we instinctively tend to think that a benevolent and loving God should not allow it. Some people presume God is either unable or unwilling to come to the aid of His people, and it warps their image of Him. But Plantinga argues that there is no such contradiction in the coexistence of God's love and power with evil if—and this is the key—*God has a good reason for allowing the evil.*

We may be confused and even outraged as we witness evil and lawlessness and the problems they create. Yet someday we may see clearly what God accomplished in us and through us because He led us through the valley of the shadow of death instead of giving us a convenient detour. We tend to forget that we are incapable of seeing into the mind of God and fully understanding His ways: "'For My thoughts are not your thoughts, nor are your ways My ways,' says the LORD. 'For as the heavens are higher than the earth, so are My ways higher than your ways, and My thoughts than your thoughts'" (Isaiah 55:8–9).

Choosing to work through the sufferings and evils in this "vale of tears" can make all the difference in the world. Even though God has not yet removed the influence of evil from humanity, He does not leave us helpless. Paul writes in Romans, "We know that all things work together for good to those who love God, to those who are the called according to His purpose" (Romans 8:28).

God does not miraculously spare His people from experiencing unpleasant circumstances in life. Instead, He miraculously helps them endure disappointments and tragedies, enabling them to eventually look back and see positive results. This promise is not to everyone but "to those who love God." Choosing to maintain a growing relationship with God is important at all times, but it will become all the more so as lawlessness increases and evil spreads its influence.

What Is God Waiting For?

Even after we concede that God may have a purpose for allowing us to endure difficulties that result from the evils in this world, the next pressing question for many of us is, For how much longer? Surely He sees that things are getting out of hand down here. We have biblical assurance that He is going to completely conquer all evil forces and redeem His world one day. It is a sure thing, a done deal. What is He waiting for?

We want God to judge the Eichmanns, the Hitlers, the ISIS militants and others who so blatantly exhibit evil and lawlessness. God is well aware of the evil in our world. In fact, it bothers Him much more than it does any of us. Because He is a perfectly holy being, sin is more abhorrent to Him than it can ever be to us. He created the people who have chosen evil, and they have the same offer of love, forgiveness and a growing relationship with Him . . . but they have turned away. Still, God has not given up on humanity just yet.

We would do well to acknowledge, like Yehiel Dinur, that Eichmann is in all of us. We all are influenced and tainted by evil more than we realize, so we need to take caution in asking God to judge evil once and for all. Most of us have family members, close friends and perhaps even prodigal children or spouses who have not yet found the only possible remedy for evil in Jesus Christ. At times we may even catch ourselves thinking, *I know I have my faults, but I'm not as bad as most of the people I know.* That may be true, but we need to remember that God will not be grading on a curve when Christ returns to judge the world. People are still putting their faith in Him every day, so we need to resist a rush to judgment. As we wait, we can do everything possible to strengthen our own faith and set a better example for those around us.

Peter's second letter makes a couple of important observations regarding the timing of God's judgment. The first is that judgment is definitely coming:

> Scoffers will come in the last days, walking according to their own lusts, and saying, "Where is the promise of His coming? For since the fathers fell asleep, all things continue as they were from the beginning of creation." For this they willfully forget: that by the word of God the heavens were of old, and the earth standing out of water and in the water, by which the world that

then existed perished, being flooded with water. But the heavens and the earth which are now preserved by the same word, are reserved for fire until the day of judgment and perdition of ungodly men.

2 Peter 3:3–7

According to Peter, the clock is ticking. Even as more time passes and more people scoff at those who are trusting God, the day is getting closer. Peter also reminds us of a previous time when evil became so rampant that God finally stepped in to deal with it. After His judgment in Noah's day, only eight people survived. We should not take lightly our tendency to rush to judgment, which brings up Peter's second point:

But, beloved, do not forget this one thing, that with the Lord one day is as a thousand years, and a thousand years as one day. The Lord is not slack concerning His promise, as some count slackness, but is longsuffering toward us, not willing that any should perish but that all should come to repentance.

2 Peter 3:8–9

What is God waiting for? He is not postponing judgment out of ignorance, neglect, apathy or any number of other reasons that people accuse Him of. Rather, He is biding His time because of His great love and mercy. He is patiently waiting for more of His hard-hearted and thick-headed human creations to come around, see how much He loves them and respond to His grace. Like the father in the Parable of the Prodigal Son, He is keeping His eye out for every person willing to come to his or her senses and approach with a humble heart. When life in our unfair and lawless world becomes too much to bear, He is always ready to take back a prodigal child.

Learning to Wait

God's timetable is usually quite different from ours. As soon as He promises something, we want results. Yet sometimes there can be quite an interlude between the giving of the promise and its fulfillment.

After God told Abraham that he would have a son, 25 years passed before the patriarch saw the birth of Isaac. During that time, Abraham (and Sarah) tried a number of things to hasten God along. Their decision to have Abraham father a son by Sarah's handmaid, Hagar, did indeed result in a son—but not the child God had intended for them to have together. In fact, the birth of Ishmael resulted in such household strife that Hagar and the boy had to leave Abraham's household twice. God protected them in the wilderness, but the rivalry between Ishmael's descendants (the Arabs) and Isaac's descendants (the Jews) continues to this day (see Genesis 16; 21:1–21).

Whenever we are waiting for God to do something He has promised, we should use that time to get closer to Him and try to better appreciate what He is doing. Specifically, as we wait for Him to take action to ultimately conquer and abolish evil, we should become more aware of situations in which *we* are able to step in and do something to lessen the evil in our spheres of influence. Instead of hiding and cowering in fear, hoping for immediate divine rescue, we might see opportunities to speak out, organize against threatening forces or make a difference in any number of ways. God frequently works through faithful people to accomplish His will on earth. Someday (perhaps soon) He will step in and eradicate evil forever, but in the meantime, there is much we can do to encourage, support and enlighten those whose lives are becoming overshadowed by the influence of lawlessness and the forces of evil.

Later chapters will deal more completely with the man of lawlessness, the intensity of the struggle as time winds down and what the future holds for those who remain faithful—as well as for those who do not. With the knowledge that evil existed before humanity did and will only get worse, we must never forget that Christ will eventually reign victorious. It does no good to worry, fear or withdraw. We need to have confidence in our Lord, trust Him to see us through the lawlessness now and to come and combat it as He leads us.

3

Lawlessness in America: A Case Study

ONE BEAUTIFUL, SUNNY SEPTEMBER MORNING, my wife and I were on a flight from New York City to Los Angeles. Shortly after takeoff, as we looked out the window and spotted the Twin Towers of the World Trade Center, we noticed one of them was on fire. Before we had traveled far, the pilot was directed to land immediately, so he diverted the plane to Detroit. Even as we neared the runway, we were still unaware of what had taken place in New York, Washington, D.C., and Pennsylvania.

Finally a passenger behind us turned on her cell phone; seconds later she announced that terrorists had flown two passenger planes into the World Trade Center. It was the moment that would forever change the nation, Americans' sense of security and our worldview.

Like millions of Americans, my wife and I were flooded with conflicting thoughts as soon as we heard the news. We were immediately concerned about the safety of our fourteen-year-old daughter, who attended high school near New York City. When her school was canceled, she had to wait at a friend's house for word of our safety. We were unable to get a message through to her for several hours. She was all right, although we soon discovered how many thousands of others were not as fortunate. Among them was the father of my daughter's best friend, a New York firefighter who courageously entered the towers as others fled. His remains were never found; they remain on hallowed ground.

All of us who are old enough remember that day, and most of us who live near New York have stories to tell of lost friends to accompany our shattered sense of security. The date 9/11 ingrained itself in hearts and minds all over the world. We are different because of what took place that day. New York—especially Ground Zero—is forever changed . . . not only physically, but also spiritually. Americans had seen and heard about terrorist attacks in other countries, but 9/11 was the first significant one by foreign terrorists against Americans on American soil. The nation changed—the hedge of protection was breached. It was a warning that the spirit of lawlessness had escalated to an entirely new level.

A History of Lawlessness

While it is natural to point our fingers at attacks such as this and blame circumstances originating outside our country, we Americans would be naïve to believe that the United States was free of the spirit of lawlessness until 9/11. We are proud to be an example for the rest of the world of a country founded on morality . . . justice . . . law . . . even Christian principles. And while that is true to a large extent, we tend to look at our history with blinders.

Americans reflect on the formation of our country with noble sentiment. We began as a refuge for unconventional Christianity when European religion became too intolerant, as various groups migrated to America to seek freedom they could not find at home (although some, such as the Puritans, brought rather harsh and restrictive laws with them). Later, when the British king imposed what the colonists saw as unjust taxes, they elected democracy over monarchy, even though they would have to fight for it. They boldly and courageously decided to establish their own agreed-upon laws, rather than blindly complying with the demands of the British figurehead. From the beginning of our birth as a nation, we Americans have attempted to be a people of law and order.

From the beginning, however, America has had its problems developing laws and civil structure. Its early emphasis on the rule of law did not immediately impose order on the land.

The Wild West

The establishment of permanent settlements in the colonies brought a pressing need for new laws:

> Outlawry in America appeared soon after the settlers had erected their first blockhouse. In New England a "Body of Laws" was enacted to combat the widespread activities of the road agents. For a first offense, a highwayman had the letter "B" branded on his forehead. The second offense brought another branding and a severe whipping; the third offense meant death. For a crime committed on the Lord's Day, his ears were cut off as additional penalty.[1]

What began as European outposts quickly became more or less civilized colonies, but those were but dots on an enormous landmass. Not even a generation after the colonies, having extracted themselves from British rule, established a viable legal system all their own, the Louisiana Purchase of 1803 doubled the size of the young nation. Americans moved west faster than the legal system could keep up.

Many of the first to go were either more adventurous than most or trying to escape something (such as arrest or creditors). They were not by nature the most law-abiding segment of the population.

When we talk of the Wild West, we mean not wilderness wild but lawless wild—disorder, violence, fighting, and killing; we mean not the grandeur of untamed nature but the drama of undisciplined and untamed men.... In addition to the existing social conditions there was the weakness of the law. It had not been designed to fit the needs of such a wild land. Water, range, and homesteading rights were outstanding examples. These laws were inadequate and the men of the West could not abide by them and survive.[2]

As a result, the history of America's western frontier is rife with stories of "frontier justice"—a less-than-ideal system to deal with offenders where lawmen were few and far between. The system included hanging judges, lynch mobs, settling disputes in gunfights and other rather barbaric means.

Yet there was an underlying understanding that people living in proximity—even in the "Wild West"—needed a degree of civility. To offset lawlessness, many rough-around-the-edges cowboys began to abide by an unwritten set of rules; thus it was outlaw activity and the frontier justice mentality that gave rise to the Code of the West.

It is difficult to find a definitive list of the "rules" in the code; a good summary, however, is provided by James P. Owen, who wanted to promote the value of the code in his own modern-day profession, investment management consulting. He includes guidelines such as "Live each day with courage," "Talk less and say more," and "Remember that some things are not for sale."[3] Other lists contain matters of etiquette that are considerably folksier, such as, "Never pass anyone on the trail without saying 'Howdy,'" or, "No matter how tired and worn out you are at the end of the day, your horse's needs come first."

The Code of the West essentially boiled down to the Golden Rule. Owen explains it well:

> Under the cattle country definition of fair play, a deal was a deal, a handshake was as good as a written contract, and there was no such thing as reneging on a debt. . . . On the open range, cowboys shared a way of life that was as difficult and tenuous as it was rewarding. So they had a natural self-interest in honoring the Code's insistence on fair play. For them, the Golden Rule was not something learned in Sunday school. The principle of "do unto others what you would have them do unto you" was nothing more and nothing less than a key to survival.[4]

Of course, given enough time, the best of systems begin to deteriorate. Eventually the Code of the West became, for many, little more than justification for any number of hostilities or crimes in an ongoing power struggle.

> In . . . straightforward activities and transactions the code worked well for both sides. When differences of opinion or disputes arose, however, the cowman tended to change his definition of the code. Taking matters into his own hands, he rationalized his behavior as following a code, but this time the code was distinctly one-sided. Now the emphasis was on might rather than right. Property—legitimately owned or not—took precedence over people.[5]

Slavery

Meanwhile, back in the (supposedly) more civilized portions of the United States, the Golden Rule was all but ignored in matters of policy. Slavery—which had existed in America since 1619, when twenty Africans were sold to the Jamestown colony—continued to burgeon because cheap human labor was so profitable. In far too many cases slaves were perceived more as property than as human beings, and all manner of atrocities were carried out by heartless and greedy slave owners. Ultimately this society-approved violation of African slaves and their descendants led to the American Civil War—resulting in more than 752,000 battle deaths, many more awful injuries and a national division that took decades to resolve. The healing is still not complete.

Treatment of Native Americans

African slaves were not the only ones who suffered cruelty and humiliation as a result of a rapidly growing nation. Native Americans soon found themselves in the path of western expansion. Some tribes attempted to assimilate into European culture; in the Southeast, for example, many tribes quickly adapted to the customs and dress of the European immigrants, and the Choctaw, Chickasaw, Seminole, Creek and Cherokee peoples became known as "the five civilized tribes." But the newcomers felt entitled to tribal lands and began to impinge by theft of property, squatting, burning and looting and other means.

Even after the Supreme Court ruled that the native tribes were sovereign nations that did not have to comply with state laws, the ruling was ignored, and a movement intensified to have the natives removed. Andrew Jackson was instrumental in the process, signing the Indian Removal Act in 1830, which paved the way during the next decade for the expulsion of tens of thousands of natives from their homes. The forced passage on the notorious Trail of Tears, a 1,200-mile trek to what is now Oklahoma, led to thousands of Native American deaths from starvation and disease, after they had been made powerless by being deprived of their rights—all so white settlers could grow cotton on millions of acres of their real estate.[6]

Other tribes farther west attempted isolation on their reservations, but the legal system continued to fail them. Treaties were broken as soon as they were written, prompting frequent conflicts and ongoing bitterness.

Human Law versus God's Law

Let's break from this historical review to reflect on the double standard that was developing. Americans during this time tended to take pride in belonging to a Christian, God-fearing nation. Many slave owners were churchgoing people. Soldiers who evicted Native American families from their homelands were following orders. The justification for such great atrocities was that these actions and attitudes fell within the law of the land. Why is it that, in a country founded with a great respect for the rule of law, whose leaders intentionally drew on Judeo-Christian morality to form the basis of national law, so many unjust laws were passed and unlawful actions abounded?

The answer is that lawlessness has little to do with civil or national law. This is because lawlessness is not the action of violating the established laws of a nation; lawlessness runs much deeper and is by nature *spiritual*. The motivations that lead man to harm his fellow man or elevate one race above another have the same source: none other than Satan himself, whom Jesus referred to as "a murderer from the beginning, [who] does not stand in the truth, because there is no truth in him" (John 8:44).

Even when people try to create just and equitable laws, problems always crop up, because human law is inadequate to deal with the spirit of lawlessness. Some of those problems are more indefensible than others. In the case of slavery, for example, the laws were written to favor the white owners. Slaves were not respected enough to be given a vote in the matter, and little consideration was given to the irrationality of slaves being expected to abide by one-sided laws in which they had no voice. The Native Americans, even after doing everything in their power to live peacefully with European "intruders," suffered the injustice of unfair laws.

What was true in the early days of American history is also true in our day: People live under a religious spirit, which is a counterfeit of the workings and power of the Holy Spirit. The religious spirit lulls people with a sense of having satisfied the law while keeping them from discovering and rooting out the spirit of lawlessness that lies beneath. This is why we are told to "not believe every spirit, but test the spirits, whether they are of God" (1 John 4:1). As we consider the problem of lawlessness in today's world, then, we must address the defiance people show toward *God's* Law. Thanks to Jesus, we have a ready summary of that Law in the most basic terms. When challenged to define the greatest commandment from the Law, He had a ready answer:

> "You shall love the LORD your God with all your heart, with all your soul, and with all your mind." This is the first and great commandment. And the second is like it: "You shall love your neighbor as yourself." On these two commandments hang all the Law and the Prophets.
>
> Matthew 22:37–40

Of all the laws of the Torah that He could have chosen, Jesus went straight to Deuteronomy 6:5 and Leviticus 19:18, pairing love for God with love for neighbor and weaving them into the same great commandment. The early Church understood the inseparable relationship between loving God and loving one another. John made it clear in one of his letters:

55

If someone says, "I love God," and hates his brother, he is a liar; for he who does not love his brother whom he has seen, how can he love God whom he has not seen? And this commandment we have from Him: that he who loves God must love his brother also.

1 John 4:20–21

Far too many people miss that connection. We say (and perhaps truly believe) that we love God, but our treatment of one another surely does not bear out our profession of love. That was one of Jesus' complaints against the Pharisees. They had reduced their Scriptures into 613 distinct laws—248 "dos" and 365 "don'ts." They took great pride in upholding all of those laws (supposedly), but Jesus boldly pointed out that they were missing Number 1 and Number 2:

Woe to you, scribes and Pharisees, hypocrites! For you pay tithe of mint and anise and cummin, and have neglected the weightier matters of the law: justice and mercy and faith. These you ought to have done, without leaving the others undone. Blind guides, who strain out a gnat and swallow a camel!

Matthew 23:23–24

The corrosive and destructive spirit of lawlessness is not primarily a consequence of defying human law. As we have seen, and will soon see further, many of those laws need to be challenged, defeated and completely transformed. The far greater threat for people is lawlessness in regard to God's Law of love. It is quite possible (and all too common) for people to be model, law-abiding citizens with regard to the laws on the courthouse books, but if they do not have genuine love for God and for "neighbor," then they are contributing to the problem of lawlessness.

Even those who accede to Jesus' priorities of love for God and love for neighbor may tend to look for loopholes. Such was the case with a lawyer Jesus confronted one day. He, too, was testing Jesus, and he asked Him outright, "And who is my neighbor?" (Luke 10:29). In response, Jesus told the familiar Parable of the Good Samaritan, expanding the definition of "neighbor" beyond what was previously thought:

> "A certain man went down from Jerusalem to Jericho, and fell among thieves, who stripped him of his clothing, wounded him, and departed, leaving him half dead. Now by chance a certain priest came down that road. And when he saw him, he passed by on the other side. Likewise a Levite, when he arrived at the place, came and looked, and passed by on the other side. But a certain Samaritan, as he journeyed, came where he was. And when he saw him, he had compassion. So he went to him and bandaged his wounds, pouring on oil and wine; and he set him on his own animal, brought him to an inn, and took care of him. On the next day, when he departed, he took out two denarii, gave them to the innkeeper, and said to him, 'Take care of him; and whatever more you spend, when I come again, I will repay you.' So which of these three do you think was neighbor to him who fell among the thieves?"
>
> And he said, "He who showed mercy on him."
>
> Then Jesus said to him, "Go and do likewise."
>
> Luke 10:30–37

Because this story has been told and retold, the word *Samaritan* produces an automatic positive response as a description of someone who goes out of his or her way to help others. But it would be hard to overemphasize how much the Jews hated Samaritans at the time Jesus told this story. He could not have chosen a more stark contrast to show that one's "neighbor" may be someone with different priorities, customs and beliefs. It is no simple matter to love such people as we love ourselves, but if our love for God is authenticated by our love for them, then we need to overcome our prejudices, fears and reluctance to reach out to those who do not look like us, talk like us or think like us. Jesus' challenge to "Go and do likewise" is not an easy one, yet it is essential if we claim to love God with all our hearts, minds and souls. And if we disregard that greatest commandment, obedience to other laws is meaningless. We have already succumbed to the destructive spirit of lawlessness.

A History of Lawlessness, Continued

In nineteenth-century United States, laws were passed in an attempt to bring compromise between Native Americans and European Americans moving west. Efforts were made to effect reconstruction after the Civil War. But despite good intentions and political maneuverings, much tension and many hard feelings remained.

The nation began to pull together to some extent in the early twentieth century as America was drawn into World War I in 1917. At the time, the Great War was thought to be "the war to end all wars" because of the carnage from a war of attrition fought with modern techniques. Perhaps ten million men died on the battlefields, with twice that many wounded.[7] No one could envision worse worldwide destruction, and yet it was but a foretaste of the bloodshed wrought by the spirit of lawlessness during World War II.

The Roaring Twenties

The addition of American forces proved a turning point for the Allies in World War I. Other nations, and American citizens themselves, began to acknowledge the United States as a major world power. The war was followed by the decade known as the Roaring Twenties, but, as newspaperman Paul Sann remarked, it might have been called "the Lawless Decade." In his book by that title, he portrays many events that contributed to his critical designation: organized crime and the Saint Valentine's Day Massacre, the Leopold and Loeb murder trial, the scandalous dance crazes, the financial shenanigans of Charles Ponzi and more. The most flagrant offense of the decade, however, was the nation's callous disregard of Prohibition. According to Sann,

> This is one of the reasons—only one—why we call it the Lawless Decade. The law that had the greatest impact on the wide and wonderful land evoked the least obedience from the people. Liquor—good, bad, indifferent or deadly—flowed like a giant waterfall during the thirteen wobbly years of the thing Herbert Hoover called "an experiment . . . noble in purpose." But the bootlegger was not alone; he dealt only in the happy juice. His errands made Prohibition a sopping-wet farce, but there were many other laws ground into the dust during the vibrant and tumultuous years from the Armistice to Repeal. Criminal laws, moral laws, civil laws, social laws, political laws, religious laws—name them.[8]

The Lawless Decade ended in a crash—the stock market crash of 1929, culminating on October 29, or Black Tuesday. The frivolity of the Jazz Age abruptly ended, replaced by the harsh reality of a national economic depression. By the time America could get on its feet, it was once more marching off into world war.

Protest Movements of the 1960s

After World War II, the nation and the world continued to be caught up in warfare; the Korean War, the Vietnam War and the re-formation of the nation of Israel in 1948 exposed intensifying international tension. In the United States a sense of disillusionment was spreading among large numbers of young people resentful of the war draft and no longer content to conform to rules they did not agree with.

By the 1960s protest movements were common. Foremost among them, the civil rights movement arose in defiance of segregationist laws that had originated during Reconstruction, which were still on the books in many states. Black Americans, particularly in the South, were unapologetically treated as second-class citizens. Dr. Martin Luther King Jr. and his followers were rigorous in remaining nonviolent in their protests; in response, they were often greeted with brutal attacks and hatred. For the first time, however, through the popularization of television, America could witness the brutality firsthand. In 1964 Congress passed the Civil Rights Act, which prohibited segregation in public facilities and discrimination in employment and education. The next year saw passage of the Voting Rights Act, which removed a number of obstacles that had been used to prevent African Americans from voting.

Television also brought the Vietnam War into America's living rooms, and students of draft age arose in protest against a war they deemed unjust and even illegal. In addition to opposing the war in Vietnam, the student movements of the 1960s protested against poverty and racism. Sit-ins were common, but as time passed many of the protests became increasingly violent:

> As the decade continued, the Student Nonviolent Coordinating Committee, an organization founded by Martin Luther King, Jr. in order to promote nonviolent protest, grew increasingly militant—as did the mostly white, middle-class "New Left" . . . By the late 1960s, activist movements had also mobilized among Asian Americans, Native Americans, Chicanos and Puerto Ricans, as well as a second wave of activism among women, gay and lesbians and the disabled.[9]

The increasing violence led to tragic results. In Detroit's impoverished Virginia Park neighborhood, riots broke out in 1967 as tensions between mostly black residents and the mostly white police force erupted; 43 people were killed and nearly 1,400 buildings were burned. In 1970, a student protest at Kent State University against the United States' bombing of Cambodia turned violent when protestors began breaking windows and looting stores. The Ohio National Guard was called in to maintain order, but when protesters began throwing objects at the soldiers, they opened fire, killing four students.

The Spread of Lawlessness

The United States was founded on the rule of law; as a nation we have managed to maintain an emphasis on peace and order, with the exception of some slips and struggles along the way. The underlying presumption has been that we would iron out our problems, establish fair and equitable laws and continue to grow better and stronger. Indeed, perhaps our finest hour came after 9/11, which was an eye-opening alert that evil from outside was making its way in. We responded to our national shock by pulling together, foregoing personal concerns to help others in greater need, consoling those who had lost loved ones and rebuilding what external terrorists thought they had destroyed.

But to believe that America has somehow risen above the spirit of lawlessness that is spreading across the world is both foolish and naïve. In the years since 9/11, the pendulum has swung far in the opposite direction, revealing that this spirit has not been subdued. My nation is being torn apart by inner-city strife, the dispute over immigration, the epidemic of addiction and more. In addition, we have begun to witness a startling disregard for God's Law. Civic laws that were based on the authority of Scripture regarding matters such as abortion and same-sex marriage have been rewritten, often in the name of tolerance. What once was shocking and abhorrent to most people is now widely accepted. The threat of lawlessness from without, while still a cause for much concern, is far less frightening than the potential consequences of extended, ongoing weakening of our internal moral compass.

Aleksandr Solzhenitsyn noted this shift in values early on. In a speech delivered on July 9, 1975, he observed,

> We are approaching a major turning point in world history, in the history of civilization. . . . I could compare it only with the turning from the Middle Ages to the modern era, a shift in our civilization. It is a juncture at which settled concepts suddenly become hazy, lose their precise contours, at which our familiar and commonly used words lose their meaning, become empty shells, and methods which have been reliable for many centuries no longer work. It's the sort of turning point where the hierarchy of values which we have venerated, and which we use to determine what is important to us and what causes our hearts to beat is starting to rock and may collapse.[10]

In previous decades it required the courage of one's convictions to determine, *This is an unjust law, and I need to take a stand against it.* These days, however, our thinking appears to be much more self-centered: *This law is too restrictive to my personal freedoms, so I'm not going to abide by it.*

Road rage is a good example of this. It used to be understood that everyone must share the highways with older, slower or less hurried drivers. Perhaps Driver Number 1 copes with rush hour by leaving home earlier and expecting delays, but Driver Number 2 drives aggressively, cutting off Driver Number 1 and almost causing an accident. In days past, Driver Number 1 might have muttered under his breath, honked the horn, shaken his fist (or worse) and otherwise made his displeasure known. Nowadays those responses have escalated, often to frightening levels.

According to the American Safety Council, two-thirds of traffic fatalities in the United States are caused by aggressive driving. Over a recent seven-year period, road rage led to 218 murders and 12,610 injuries. Two percent of drivers actually confessed to trying to run another aggressive driver off the road, while 37 percent of aggressive-driving incidents involved a firearm.[11] This is the degree of lawlessness Americans face daily just trying to get from one place to another!

When our emotions get involved at an even deeper level, the situation only gets worse: Escalation of racial tension, distrust of police, gang activity and other violence are becoming the pattern. Time after time after time, Americans have recoiled in horror at yet another violent street crime or mass shooting. In a *Washington Post* infographic titled "The Math of Mass Shootings," you can see at a glance every one of the 874 men, women and children who have been killed in mass shootings during the past fifty years, along with their names and a brief description.[12] You can also meet the 130 shooters involved (as of July 2016) and see the 245 guns used in those deaths. Sadly, the site must be updated with regularity.

The epidemic of violence is more than a plank in a political platform or a topic for talk radio; it will not be resolved with the passage of new, tougher laws because it is not simply a civil matter. It is a symptom of the much deeper and wider spiritual problem. A major shift appears to be taking place, indicating a new and threatening level of lawlessness in the United States, from the pinnacle of government to the living rooms of every community. The consequence of widespread sin in a nation or community is something that can be seen throughout history: rampant violence.

Lawlessness Precedes Violence

Prior to the great Flood, Scripture tells us that human wickedness had gotten so bad that "the LORD was sorry that He had made man on the earth, and He was grieved in His heart" (Genesis 6:6). How was all that sin made evident? Through widespread violence: "The earth also was corrupt before God, and the earth was filled with violence" (verse 11). So God told Noah, "The end of all flesh has come before Me, for the earth is filled with violence through them; and behold, I will destroy them with the earth" (verse 13).

Hosea prophesied to Israel of the coming Assyrian invasion, which would ultimately destroy the Northern Kingdom. Maybe you can relate to his sense of isolation in a world teeming with violence: "The days of punishment have come; the days of recompense have come. Israel knows! The prophet is a fool, the spiritual man is insane, because of the greatness of your iniquity and great enmity" (Hosea 9:7). In Hosea's time genuine prophets and people committed to God were so rare that *they* were considered the crazy ones in a society of mounting hostility.

Or maybe you feel like Habakkuk more than a century later, a prophet in Judah shortly before the Babylonians descended on the nation to destroy the Temple and the city of Jerusalem:

> O LORD, how long shall I cry, and You will not hear? Even cry out to you, "Violence!" and You will not save. Why do You show me iniquity, and cause me to see trouble? For plundering and violence are before me; there is strife, and contention arises. Therefore the law is powerless, and justice never goes forth. For the wicked surround the righteous; therefore perverse judgment proceeds.
>
> Habakkuk 1:2–4

Before the great Flood . . . before the Northern Kingdom of Israel fell to the Assyrians . . . before the Southern Kingdom of Judah was crushed and driven into exile by the Babylonians . . . in every case the unbridled sin of God's people was evident from the increasing lawlessness in their societies. In each case, the great sin and violence were met with a judgment of God.

Other Scriptures make it clear that the last days will be preceded with similar (and even worse) violence throughout the world. Both Jesus (Matthew 23–24) and Paul (2 Thessalonians 2) warned of the wickedness that will intensify during the days prior to Christ's return—including wars, rebellion and other acts of violence. They both realized that people committed to God's Kingdom would be vastly outnumbered and persecuted. But never did they indicate any justification for giving up.

Jesus said, "Because lawlessness will abound, the love of many will grow cold" (Matthew 24:12). We are seeing that today, even in America. Yet He followed that statement with this: "But he who endures to the end shall be saved. And this gospel of the kingdom will be preached in all the world as a witness to all the nations, and then the end will come" (verses 13–14).

After painting a rather bleak picture of the times to come, Paul reminded his readers,

> God from the beginning chose you for salvation through sanctification by the Spirit and belief in the truth, to which He called you by our gospel, for the obtaining of the glory of our Lord Jesus Christ. Therefore, brethren, stand fast and hold the traditions which you were taught, whether by word or our epistle.
>
> 2 Thessalonians 2:13–15

As we witness the growing lawlessness and increasing violence in our nations, it is natural to feel scared . . . overpowered . . . helpless.

65

But that is exactly the time when we need to stand fast and endure to the end. We must always remember that despite being surrounded by what appears to be perpetual chaos, God is in total control. As long as we remain faithful to Him and are led and empowered by His Spirit, we have nothing to fear.

Whether or not we acknowledge the fact, America is still one nation under God. Perhaps only a small minority will continue to adhere to God's Law and make an effort to quell the lawlessness that has prevailed, but I encourage you to be one of those people. Later chapters will provide more specific strategies for responding to lawlessness, but at this point suffice it to say that giving up is never the best option.

Fight the good fight. Finish the race. Keep the faith. Your nation—and God's Kingdom—will be stronger as a result.

4

The Men of Nineveh

ONE NIGHT AS I WAS READING SCRIPTURE, one of Jesus' statements grabbed my attention:

> This is an evil generation. It seeks a sign, and no sign will be given to it except the sign of Jonah the prophet. For as Jonah became a sign to the Ninevites, so also the Son of Man will be to this generation. . . . The men of Nineveh will rise up in the judgment with this generation and condemn it.
>
> Luke 11:29–30, 32

Who are these "men of Nineveh"? How are they going to judge and condemn this evil generation? In other words, what was Jesus telling us about the future?

This is an important question for all who are alive today, because we are drawing closer to the end of the age and the appearance of the man of lawlessness (see 2 Thessalonians 2:7–8). This means we are also coming closer to the judgment of "this evil generation," and we may even see signs of its beginning. Before we try to answer the question, though, we need to figure out who Jesus was referring to when He said, "This is an evil generation." He speaks of "this generation" again in Matthew 24:29–35, where He clearly refers to the generation that will be alive when He returns. The phrase *this generation* is used often in connection with the end of the age before the return of the Lord. Dr. Darrell Bock, research professor of New Testament studies at Dallas Theological Seminary, adds additional insight:

> Another, slightly more likely way to take the verse is to see the reference to "generation" not as chronological in force, but moral or ethical. So this "evil" generation, which is what the unredeemed creation consists of, will not pass away until Jesus returns. Such a use of "generation" occurs in Luke 9:41 and 11:29.[1]

One traditional view of Luke 11:32 is that the ancient men of Nineveh will be called to the judgment before the great white throne (Revelation 20:11–12) to testify against those who reject the message of the Gospel. At first glance this makes sense, until we realize that nowhere in Scripture are we told that God will call or need witnesses to testify against the accused. God alone knows what is in the human heart (see John 2:24–25).

Upon further study and reflection, I believe that these men of Nineveh will make a "prophetic" entrance—similar in substance but different in appearance—prior to the return of Christ. Just as Jonah was a sign to the people of Nineveh to repent before the coming judgment of God, the appearance of the men of Nineveh is a sign to repent before the coming of the man of lawlessness (the Antichrist). But what will they look like, and what will they do? To fully understand how the men of Nineveh will bring condemnation on this evil generation, we have to take a look back to the

Nineveh that the people of Jesus' day understood: the capital of the mighty and brutal kingdom of Assyria.

The Significance of Nineveh

Whenever Nineveh is mentioned, most people first think of Jonah's reluctant encounter with the Ninevites. After proclaiming, "Yet forty days, and Nineveh shall be overthrown!" (Jonah 3:4), Jonah watched as they believed God, repented and turned from their evil way (see verses 5–10). Though their hearts were opened to God in this instance, the rest of their history gives a different picture.

We saw in chapter 2 that Nimrod, the same figure who established Babel (Babylon), also founded the city of Nineveh (Genesis 10:8–12), which makes it one of the world's oldest cities. Unlike Babylon, which retained its reputation throughout the ups and downs of history, Nineveh was almost forgotten after its destruction in 612 BC, until its ruins underneath the Iraqi city of Mosul were excavated in the first half of the nineteenth century.

As Assyria grew into an empire, Nineveh was showing its age. But when Sennacherib came to power (704–681 BC), he decided to make Nineveh the showcase of all Assyrian cities. To that end, he established it as the capital city and built himself a grand residence. His home was known as "Palace without a Rival," an impressive edifice bedecked with ivory and various ornamental woods (maple, cedar, cypress, spruce and others). Of more interest to contemporary archaeologists are the artwork and written records that have been uncovered in the palace.

Babylon and Assyria were both powerful nations with extended influence. The relationship between them was a tenuous one, with the balance of power shifting back and forth:

[Nineveh] was for many years the capital of the great Assyrian empire, and its fortunes ebbed and flowed with the long strife between Babylonia and Assyria. Of the two kingdoms, or empires, Babylonia was the more cultured but Assyria the more warlike. The kingdom over which Nineveh and its kings long ruled was north of Babylon and more in the hills, and these facts made more for warlikeness than the more sedentary culture of a warmer climate.[2]

As the capital of Assyria, Nineveh was the seat of kings such as Sennacherib, Ashurnasirpal, Ashurbanipal and others. Their war records, which have survived to this day, reveal a stunning and stomach-turning level of violence against their enemies. According to one source,

> The army rarely moved out in full force or engaged in large battles in the open field. Its tactic was often one of terrorizing the enemy into submission. Territories were approached with massive forces and, if they did not yield immediately, cities and villages that presented easy targets were attacked. When conquered, the inhabitants were severely punished as examples. They were tortured, raped, beheaded, and flayed, and their corpses, heads, or skins were publicly displayed. Houses were razed, fields were covered with salt, and orchards cut down.[3]

In 612 BC the Babylonians (accompanied by the armies of the Scythians and Medes) came rolling in and destroyed Nineveh, seemingly once and for all. Although it was common for invading armies to take over existing cities when possible to spare the effort and expense of building new ones, that was not the case in this instance:

> Most of the Assyrian heartland's population was resettled in Babylonia where Nabopolassar and his successor Nebuchadnezzar

transformed their capital Babylon into an imperial centre to rival its Assyrian prototypes in Kalhu, Dur-Sarrukin, and Nineveh. No one took over the maintenance of these cities, whose enormous size and population could only be upheld with extensive and expensive regional irrigation systems supporting the fresh water supply. Without upkeep, the canals and aqueducts soon became dilapidated, never to be used again. At Nineveh, the bodies of those killed defending the city were never cleared away, as gruesome discoveries at Nineveh's Halzi Gate illustrate. At Kalhu, bodies of executed men were dumped in the well providing the citadel with drinking water, which illustrates a desire to destroy and spoil, rather than appropriate, the Assyrian heartland.[4]

As mighty as it had been, Assyria was not to recover. Nineveh settled into the dust of Iraq, forgotten for millennia until being rediscovered in the mid-1800s.

Will the Ninevites who repented at the preaching of Jonah be in heaven with us someday? That is for God to decide. As far as we can tell, Jonah's message said nothing of salvation or eternity. He gave them a terse warning and they responded—perhaps more out of fear and self-interest than for any other reason. Still, God relented from bringing disaster on the city and later used Assyria as an instrument of judgment against Northern Israel (2 Chronicles 33:10–13).

A clear indication that the Ninevite "repentance" was short lived is seen in the book of Nahum, which is a forecast of the coming destruction of Nineveh. Several years after Jonah's mission, God's message to the Ninevites had changed: "'Behold, I am against you,' says the LORD of hosts, 'I will burn your chariots in smoke, and the sword shall devour your young lions; I will cut off your prey from the earth, and the voice of your messengers shall be heard no more'" (Nahum 2:13). At about the same time the prophet Zephaniah was promoting a similar message: "And [the Lord] will stretch out His hand against the north, destroy Assyria, and make Nineveh a desolation, as dry as the wilderness" (Zephaniah 2:13).[5]

This is why I find it so intriguing that Jesus stated, "The men of Nineveh *will rise up* in the judgment with this generation and condemn it" (Luke 11:32, emphasis mine). Clearly He was directing His listeners to look back to ancient Nineveh's response to Jonah as a striking example of what can happen for anyone who hears and obeys God's Word. Because Nineveh was eventually destroyed, however, is there not also a prophetic significance to what Jesus was saying? In addition to calling us to follow the Ninevites' example of repentance, I think Jesus was also alerting us to look *forward*, to a time when Nineveh would literally "rise up" in a time of judgment.

In fact, I believe that we are living in that time, and that these prophetic men of Nineveh have *already* appeared, in similar form to their historical predecessors: They have followed a long history of almost incomprehensible cruelty displayed in ancient Assyria, boasting of the extent of brutality they show toward those they deem to be enemies. In their quest to expand their power, they overtook the modern city that lies atop the ancient ruins of Nineveh, declaring the dominion of their religious form of government and establishing that city as their cultural capital. Empowered by the spirit of lawlessness present in Nineveh from its earliest days, they have attempted to spread their influence far beyond its borders.

Who are these prophetic men of Nineveh? I believe they are none other than ISIS.

Before I give reasons for this, I want to explain why the spirit that was present in ancient Nineveh has the power to influence modern-day culture. The power and proclamation of the Gospel in the Middle East have been in steady decline for centuries. The

Church has lost its ability to influence and transform culture and allowed the enemy to infiltrate all facets of society. Instead of binding the strong man (Luke 11:21–22), the evil power behind Nineveh and the rest of the Middle East has been free to roam—and expand.

When Christians do not preach the Gospel, they incur judgment; in the Middle East, the result has been the crushing of Christianity under the weight of Islam. With that in mind, the passage in Luke takes on new relevance:

> [Jesus] began to say, "This is an evil generation. It seeks a sign, and no sign will be given to it except the sign of Jonah the prophet. For as Jonah became a sign to the Ninevites, so also the Son of Man will be to this generation. The queen of the South will rise up in the judgment with the men of this generation and condemn them, for she came from the ends of the earth to hear the wisdom of Solomon; and indeed a greater than Solomon is here. The men of Nineveh will rise up in the judgment with this generation and condemn it, for they repented at the preaching of Jonah; and indeed a greater than Jonah is here.
>
> Luke 11:29–32

On one level, Jesus was chiding the generation of people that was rejecting Him. He contrasted their lack of spiritual insight with surprising acknowledgments of God's power from the Queen of Sheba and even the Ninevites, who were not prone to repentance or humility. Yet both the Queen of Sheba and the Ninevites had responded to God's message, which put the first-century Jewish leaders to shame. That lesson from this passage has always been apparent. Yet after my research on the men of Nineveh, it was just as plain to me that Jesus was speaking to my generation as well. It could not have been clearer if He had said, "The men of Nineveh will rise up in the judgment with this generation and condemn it—and they shall be called ISIS."

The Men of Nineveh: Then and Now

The Islamic State has been on the rise for some time. Although its forces have faltered somewhat in Syria and Iraq, they have much larger territory in their sights:

> The Islamic State's strategy is both local and global. The group pursues interlocking campaigns across multiple geographic areas: Its local strategy in Iraq and Syria is to remain in control of terrain as a caliphate, while its regional strategy is to expand that caliphate across the Middle East by incorporating more fighting groups, which will allow it to further destabilize states and gain control of more terrain. Its global strategy, meanwhile, is to set the conditions for an apocalyptic war with the West, first and foremost by polarizing societies to be for or against Islam.[6]

There is compelling evidence that the Ninevites of ancient Assyria have a connection with ISIS in the number of uncanny similarities between the two groups. One clear connection has to do with geography. Though Nineveh had been a great and powerful capital, it disappeared from history after its fall in the seventh century BC. For more than two thousand years, its ruins lay forgotten beneath the dust of the desert. In the nineteenth century, they were discovered within the limits of the Iraqi city of Mosul—and since June 2014 Mosul has been a stronghold for ISIS. As of this writing, the Iraqi army, with support from other nations, is attempting to expel ISIS from Mosul, which ISIS regards as both strategically and spiritually important (more on that later). Whether or not they are successful, the fact that ISIS has expanded its worldwide reach since its capture of Mosul is an indication of the spirit behind it—the same spirit that compelled the ancient Ninevites. Let's look at a few other similarities.

A Passion for Violence

Assyria was a surprisingly cultured place. They are credited with first dividing a circle into 360 degrees, inventing flushing toilets and locks and keys, and establishing the first postal system, libraries, paved roads and aqueducts.[7] Yet, as we have seen, they were also incredibly brutal:

> [The Assyrians] created the world's first great army, and the world's first great empire. This was held together by two factors: their superior abilities in siege warfare, and their reliance on sheer, unadulterated terror. It was Assyrian policy always to demand that examples be made from those who resisted them; this included deportations of entire peoples and horrific physical punishments. One inscription from a temple in the city of Nimrod records the fate of the leaders of the city of Suru on the Euphrates River, who rebelled from and were reconquered by King Ashurbanipal (668–626 BC). "I buil[t] a pillar at the city gate, and I flayed all the chief men who had revolted, and I covered the pillar with their skins: some I walled-up inside the pillar, some I impaled upon the pillar on stakes." Such punishments were not uncommon.[8]

Fast-forward to the same part of the world today. Media reports from the ongoing wars in the Middle East are both graphic and disturbing. One would have hoped that in the course of 2,600 years or so, the Assyrians' historical reputation for savagery would have given way to more civilized, humane treatment of others. But unfortunately, current reports are disturbingly similar. When we think they surely can do nothing worse than the abduction and detention of religious minorities, forced marriage, public behead-ings and unthinkable sexual abuse of helpless victims, they continue to shock. An Iraqi refugee from Mosul who witnessed fighting between local troops and ISIS militants reported seeing a "row of decapitated soldiers and policemen" and said the victims' heads were placed in rows; this has become a savage ISIS trademark.[9]

The biggest difference, however, is that ISIS exhibits such detest-able behavior against innocent and helpless victims. The violent actions of the ancient Assyrian leaders, at least, were primarily directed toward opponents who had gone to war on the battle-field and lost, and who would likely do something similar had the outcome been different.

As this is being written, reports have surfaced that ISIS members publicly burned nineteen young Yazidi girls to death for refusing to have sex with the militants. When in August 2014 ISIS took control of the Yazidi region of northern Iraq, almost forty thousand people were displaced. It is believed that more than three thou-sand Yazidi girls were taken as sex slaves. Others remain trapped on Mount Sinjar and reportedly have suffered mass killings, rape and kidnappings.[10]

Nor is ISIS brutality limited to the Middle East. Michael Mc-Caul, chairman of the Homeland Security Committee in the U.S. House of Representatives, made this observation at a recent hearing:

The past month we witnessed four major terrorist attacks, in four weeks, in four countries, including the deadliest attack on the U.S. homeland since 9/11. All of these attacks are believed to be the work of ISIS, the new standard-bearer of evil. In fact, the group has now been linked to almost 100 plots against the West since 2014—an unprecedented wave of terror. Nearly fifteen years after 9/11, we must confront the reality that we are not winning the war against Islamist terror. While groups like ISIS may be losing some ground in Syria and Iraq, overall they are not "on the run," as the Obama Administration says. They are on the rise. But I am concerned that we have only seen the tip of the iceberg.[11]

Fanatic Devotion to Their God

The primary Assyrian god was Assur, whose name was reflected in numerous geographic locations and names of their kings. (The name *Assyria* is a Greek variation that loses the original meaning: "Land of Assur.") There was also a city of Assur, the original center of the nation and origin of its leaders. A temple to Assur was in the city of Assur, so the god and the city became inseparable.[12]

The violence inflicted on enemies was attributed to the power of Assur, just as any failure on the part of an Assyrian leader (such as a military defeat) was seen as an abandonment by the god. An old adage often attributed to Winston Churchill (and others) maintains that "history is written by the victors"; the record keeping of the Assyrians lends support to that statement. When examining Assyrian reliefs, you will never see that the Assyrians lost a battle or even that an Assyrian soldier was ever wounded or killed—a symbol of the benevolence of the gods on the Assyrian kings.[13]

As a radical Islamic movement, ISIS shares the same fanaticism in their devotion to their god. Their purpose in engaging in military activity is infused with religious meaning: to establish strict Islamic government in the areas under their control. Only when ISIS took control of Mosul, the modern-day city of Nineveh, did they declare their territory to be an Islamic caliphate, and Mosul is so important to ISIS that they consider it a "crown jewel" of their realm.[14]

One practice of the Assyrians to add insult to injury after a crushing defeat of an enemy was to attempt a divine (and psychological) domination: They collected cult statues of the gods of their enemies and placed them in the temple of Assur. It was a subtle but effective tactic:

> The statues of gods were seen as manifestations of the deities, and by staying as Assur's guests, or hostages, in his home, these gods accepted, for all to see, Assur's sovereignty. . . . [Enemies] found themselves deserted by their gods who moreover seemed to recognize Assur as their host and overlord. The strategy of god-napping was designed to persuade enemies or reluctant allies to follow their deities' lead and to accept Assyrian domination. It was often successful.[15]

So successful were the Assyrians at this strategy that they had to compile the "Divine Directory of Assur," a quite lengthy list (still available for examination) of the collected sacred statues of their enemies that filled the temple.

(You might recall that the Philistines attempted a similar tactic after they captured Israel's Ark of the Covenant in a battle. They placed it in the temple of their god, Dagon. But after finding Dagon broken and facedown before the Ark two days straight, they wisely decided to return it to Israel as quickly as possible; see 1 Samuel 5.)

ISIS has adapted this strategy: Rather than collecting sacred artifacts from other religions, they are bent on either selling them off for profit or destroying them. Looting religious sites has already reportedly made them tens of millions of dollars from the sale of invaluable books, Roman mosaics, clay tablets and other works of art. What they cannot conveniently sell, they heartlessly destroy with bulldozers and explosives. Wherever they are in control, there is little hope for art museums, temples, ancient Christian churches and other irreplaceable artifacts and buildings.

Mosul itself had been considered the center of the Assyrian Church of the East because several tombs of Old Testament prophets lay there, including the tomb of Jonah; many have been destroyed since ISIS took control of the city.[16] And the people who want to preserve such things? In Mosul, the Christians were either killed or chased out. In Palmyra, Syria, ISIS publicly executed an archaeologist who had overseen excavations in that area for decades, then hung his headless body from a column.[17] Space does not permit going on about the atrocities committed to art and culture by ISIS—and this on top of the extraordinary human suffering they have caused.

The language related to ISIS is taking on a very apocalyptic and religious tone among politicians, the media and the general population. Discussions about the end of the world, the last days and the current state of lawlessness are preparing us for the entrance of the man of lawlessness, the Antichrist.

Pictorial Documentation of Gruesome Acts

We have seen that ancient Assyrian writings detailed numerous specific and graphic actions taken by kings and warriors after utterly conquering their enemies. Some people believe those writings started out as letters to the Assyrian gods.

Verbal descriptions of the bloody deeds committed were apparently not enough, however; Assyrian art abounds with pictures and carvings showing such disturbing scenes. In a bronze relief found near Mosul, two victims of Shalmaneser III are highlighted: one prisoner impaled on a stake and the other in custody of a soldier, missing both hands and feet. Meanwhile, numerous hands and feet are scattered across the ground, severed heads hang from the walls and flames destroy the city. Other reliefs show human heads in stacks like totem poles, people being skinned alive and no shortage of other horrific scenes.

Modern sensibilities make it difficult for many of us to understand or endorse such bloodshed. And it is exactly that innate sense of horror that motivates ISIS to use shock treatment as they go public with their most violent deeds.

No longer do vicious terrorists need to carve out their exploits on stone tablets to intimidate their peers and impress future generations. Today they use tweets and streaming video. Anonymous, hooded figures dressed in black execute hostages as the world watches. ISIS uses social media to their advantage, although many sites that cover their activity must warn of "graphic images."[18]

The internet's purpose of interconnecting people throughout the world for better communication, peace and understanding has had some negative aspects, as ISIS and other terrorist groups use the newest technologies to their advantage. Social media has done more for terrorist groups than advertise their activities to a wider audience: It has become a channel for recruitment. They can now enlist and train members in other continents without the need to travel to and from the Middle East. They can also better coordinate multiple attacks. In a recent article on the topic, the authors offered a sobering thought: "A decade ago, it would have been unthinkable that a militant in Syria might become pen pals with a lonely teenager in small-town America."[19]

The Strong Man . . . and the Stronger One

To help those living in the last days discern the times, Jesus gave prophetic declarations that would signify those times had come. One of them was His prophecy of the men of Nineveh rising up. It is important to understand that the impact of ISIS reaches far beyond Iraq and the Middle East. For one thing, prophecy fulfilled in part or completely is a source of encouragement and a tool for believers worldwide. Secondly, a global terror network that is no longer restricted to geographical borders is a new phenomenon, with implications for the entire world. Unlike with other terrorist groups, the appearance of ISIS can be directly linked to the increase of lawlessness on a global scale.

Just prior to Jesus' statement in Luke 11 about the men of Nineveh rising up, we read another insightful passage relevant to the issue of lawlessness in regard to ISIS. Jesus had cast a demon out of a mute man, enabling the man to speak at last, and His critics immediately made a brash accusation: "He casts out demons by Beelzebub, the ruler of the demons" (Luke 11:15).

Jesus responded to the accusation with a logical question: Why would Beelzebub want to cast out a demon? That would mean Satan was "divided against himself," which made no sense. Jesus then exposed Satan's strategy:

> When an unclean spirit goes out of a man, he goes through dry places, seeking rest; and finding none, he says, "I will return to my house from which I came." And when he comes, he finds it swept and put in order. Then he goes and takes with him seven other spirits more wicked than himself, and they enter and dwell there; and the last state of that man is worse than the first.
>
> Luke 11:24–26

Satan is "a strong man, fully armed" (verse 21) who wields significant authority. He oversees a vast network of demonic forces that hinder prayer, control governments, influence policy, increase crime and impede the operation of miracles. Daniel 10:13 reveals a behind-the-scenes spiritual power struggle showing how strong and evil powers (in this case, the "prince of the kingdom of Persia") interfere with human spiritual growth. A similar evil personality was identified as the "prince of Greece" (Daniel 10:20).

I believe demonic spirits are assigned geographic regions (cities, countries, etc.) of the world and wield great power. Yet Jesus makes it clear that Satan, the "strong man," is helpless against one "stronger than he" who will overcome him and reclaim everything he has acquired (Luke 11:20–23). God has given the Church the power and authority to bind these territorial spirits (Luke 9:1; 10:17), but that does not mean our success will be easy or automatic.

On at least one occasion Jesus' disciples were embarrassed and befuddled when a desperate father brought them a demon-possessed child and they were unable to cast out the spirit. When Jesus arrived, He rebuked the demon and explained to the disciples that in some cases fasting is necessary in addition to prayer. He also regularly emphasized the importance of persistence in prayer (Luke 11:1–13, for example). We dare not be too quick to give up.

Perseverance was one aspect of a 2007 speech delivered by President George W. Bush concerning U.S. involvement in Iraq (emphasis added):

> Our enemy, the enemies of freedom, love chaos. Out of that chaos they could find new safe havens. Withdrawal would have emboldened these radicals and extremists. It would have confirmed their belief that our nations were weak. It would help them gain new recruits, new resources. It would cause them to believe they could strike free nations at their choice.
>
> Withdrawal would have increased the probability that coalition troops would be forced to return to Iraq one day, and confront *an enemy that is even more dangerous*. Failure in Iraq should be unacceptable to the civilized world. The risks are enormous.[20]

President Bush correctly identified the problem, but it is a problem that will never resolve at a secular level despite our best efforts. Wars continue to be fought in Iraq and the Middle East, but the real battle is spiritual. The cold-hearted, bloodthirsty mentality of the Assyrians, surely fueled by demonic activity, eventually came to an end . . . for a time. Nineveh fell and disappeared. The house

was "swept and put in order," so to speak. But although its ⌐
of evil was put on hold, it was never replaced with the power and
goodness of a loving God. By the time Nineveh was rediscovered,
Iraq belonged to the Ottoman Empire, a world power, and the
evil that was revealed was even stronger than before. ISIS is currently one arm of "the strong man" and will continue to be a threat
until the power of Jesus Christ—the Stronger Man—ultimately
overcomes.

The Middle East has been in flux for thousands of years. While
efforts to bring peace to the Middle East are noble, the prophetic
reality is that peace will come to this region only when the King
of glory, the Lord Jesus, returns to rule as the King of kings and
Lord of lords. This truth should not deter our efforts to seek peace
and do all that we can to mitigate lawlessness in the Middle East
and around the world.

I frequently hear people resign themselves to the idea that wars
have been fought in that part of the world since the beginning of
time, and the bloodshed there will never end. I know the situation
seems hopeless at times, but we must never forget that the power
of God can provide hope in such seemingly hopeless situations.
God has shown numerous times how He can revive a nation when
His people are faithful.

One prime example is Argentina during the early 1950s, a period
when the entire country seemed to be under a cloud of darkness.
Missionaries had labored for many years with woefully few con-
verts as evidence of their efforts. But an Argentine revival began
in 1954, and by all accounts, it was the power of prevailing prayer
that broke the stronghold over Argentina. A day finally arrived
when "the ruling spirit of Argentina was bound and the strong
man of Argentina was overcome. The Lion of Judah's tribe had
again prevailed. Michael had once again come forth in battle to
help the children of the Lord."[21]

Contributing to that revival was a little-known healing evangelist named Tommy Hicks, who went to Argentina to fill in for a more prominent missionary who was unable to attend a scheduled crusade. Before long, large stadiums were filling with people in response to Hicks's preaching, prayers and healing. An estimated 300,000 people came to Christ over a period of 54 days.[22]

Nations can live in spiritual darkness for long periods of time, but when God's light begins to shine in the darkness, changes can occur surprisingly quickly. ISIS and other extremist organizations attempt to wield power through fear, terror and other threatening tactics. God's power, however, spreads through love, steadfast faith and persistent prayer.

Today's Church, now more than ever, needs to heed Jesus' call for more persistence in prayer, for fasting and other spiritual disciplines and for God's will to be done on earth as it is in heaven (Matthew 6:10). Jesus made it clear that we are living under an open heaven in which all the power of God is available and at our disposal. What a powerful idea: We are to "bind the strong man" and release heaven on earth through prayer! When we do this, we will begin to see a new wave of power, healing and joy in our homes, communities and world.

Some people are beginning to detect a glimmer of light amid the spiritual darkness of the Middle East. According to Joel C. Rosenberg,[23] although 2015 was the "worst year in modern history for Christian persecution," statistics show that a reliable estimate of ten million Muslims have converted to faith in Jesus Christ in the period between 1960 and 2010. Rosenberg's book *Epicenter*[24] presents recent events and statistics of how Christianity is gaining strength in North Africa, central Asia, Iraq, Iran and elsewhere in the Middle East. The current rate of progress might seem insignificant in light of an estimated 1.6 billion Muslims worldwide, but the numbers are increasing.

Assyria was a mighty empire indeed. But long before those powers arose to threaten God's people, David was fighting other strong forces in that part of the world. He reminds us that God is more powerful than any enemy we face, and the battle will not be over until He has claimed victory and delivered His people. As we watch the news and see the threats of today's enemies, let us affirm with the psalmist, "The LORD is my rock and my fortress and my deliverer; My God, my strength, in whom I will trust; my shield and the horn of my salvation" (Psalm 18:2).

THE END TIMES

LAWLESSNESS HAS ALWAYS BEEN A PROBLEM, from the fall of Lucifer, to Adam and Eve in the Garden, to Noah and the Flood and throughout human history. Numerous biblical writers speak of a time to come when the spirit of lawlessness will release lawlessness to exceed every previous level. In fact, they connect that rise in lawlessness with the period just before the return of Christ. Although only God the Father knows the day or hour that promise will be fulfilled (Matthew 24:36), in this section we will see that recent world events—not least among them the abhorrent levels of lawlessness we are currently witnessing—align with biblical prophecy like never before. Current conditions are such that the end times might be closer than we realize.

5

The Rise of Israel

PEOPLE WHO CHOOSE EXTREME LIFE CHANGES tend to make the news. A stockbroker cashes in his portfolio, walks away from Wall Street and starts a nonprofit to help underprivileged youth. A homemaker goes back to school to get the training she needs to start a growing business from scratch. Empty nesters forgo the security of their retirement and commit to missions work. Walking away from a sure thing to follow a less secure call gets people's attention.

Sometimes this happens early. Charles Thomas (C. T.) Studd, for example, is now known primarily as a prominent British missionary. But in the late 1800s he and his brothers were getting noticed for their skill at playing cricket. C. T. had a promising athletic career ahead of him, but after one brother suffered a serious illness, young Charles found himself weighing the benefits of "fame and flattery" against the reality of eternity. Hearing the call of God on his life, he chose instead to take the Gospel to China, India and the Belgian Congo as a missionary. Those who knew him best tried to dissuade him, but he replied, "If Jesus Christ be God and died for me, then no sacrifice can be too great for me to make for Him."[1] Upon the death of his father, Studd gave away his inheritance of £29,000 to various causes promoting the Gospel. This extreme change in life direction vastly improved the lives of countless others.

Abraham and the Promise

Other life changes, just as dramatic, occur late in life. Perhaps no life change in history was more significant than Abraham's decision, at age 75, to leave his homeland and move to a foreign country. Abraham could look back over a lifetime of accomplishment in Mesopotamia: He had a wife, flocks and herds, and he had prospered as resident of a prestigious city. Most people in Abraham's position would be looking to ride out the rest of their years with a minimum of stress or change. Perhaps Abraham would have done the same, but God intervened.

Abraham's home, the city-state of Ur, lay about 140 miles southeast of Babylon near the shores of the Persian Gulf. Modern excavations indicate it was a city of education and commerce, where ships brought gold, ivory, alabaster, hard woods and other treasures on a regular basis. But Ur was also a city of idolatry. A primary deity was the moon god, which went by a number of names, including Nanna, Su'en, and Allah ("the god"). According to historian Albert Hourani, "The Islamic name used for god was 'Allah,' which was already in use for one of the local gods."[2] And Welsh historian Witton T. Davies adds,

> Towards the end of the sixth century of our era the indigenous Arabs who had not embraced Judaism or Christianity worshiped many gods: their Sabianism, however monotheistic at the outset,

could hardly issue in anything else. In the Qaaba or sanctuary of
Mekka there were over three hundred images of gods. But at the
head of these deities was Allah, *the* God, who had his wife Allat,
just as other Semitic gods (cf. Baal and Ashtoreth) had their wives.[3]

Abraham's father had previously relocated the family to Haran—
change enough for many people. But while in Haran, Abraham
received an intriguing invitation from God:

> Get out of your country, from your family and from your father's
> house, to a land that I will show you. I will make you a great na-
> tion; I will bless you and make your name great; and you shall be a
> blessing. I will bless those who bless you, and I will curse him who
> curses you; and in you all the families of the earth shall be blessed.
>
> Genesis 12:1–3

Would that offer have been enough to entice you to rise from
your Sumerian La-Z-Boy and head west? After all, God did not
even reveal Abraham's destination. The decision to move required
an immense level of trust and faith. And not only was Abraham
asked to leave his home, he was also expected to renounce his gods.
Only a divine encounter with the living God, the true God, could
have brought about such a change.

But one thing may have been especially appealing to Abraham:
God's promise to "make you a great nation." Abraham was, so far,
childless; perhaps he was eager to become a true patriarch—not
just a wealthy old man. Whatever his reasoning, he packed up and
left. His obedience to this command would result in a blessing to
all people.

Abraham's unquestioning response says a lot about him. And
the invitation says a lot about God. What kind of God chooses
an unknown senior citizen, living in a remote dot on the map, to

be the carrier of the message of redemption for the whole world? The same kind of God who loved all humanity enough to send His only Son as a vulnerable baby, born in another small, insignificant spot on the globe. God loves to use those who are weak and seemingly irrelevant in order to confound the wise and bring Him glory (1 Corinthians 1:26–29).

Too many believers settle for less than what God wants to provide them. We want to know God's will for our lives . . . to a point. But we grow complacent with form over power. We experience God's salvation and then stop seeking out the deeper things of God. Not Abraham! He learned, long before the author of Hebrews, that God "is a rewarder of those who diligently seek Him" (Hebrews 11:6). Abraham was diligent and, as we are about to see, he was rewarded for it. Pastor and author Bill Johnson has said, "If you live cautiously, your friends will call you wise. You just won't move many mountains."[4]

So, in pursuit of the reward, Abraham made the long and arduous journey from Mesopotamia to what we now know as Israel. Within a short time, He began to reveal His intentions about the land He had promised to show Abraham:

> Lift your eyes now and look from the place where you are—northward, southward, eastward, and westward; for all the land which you see I give to you and your descendants forever. And I will make your descendants as the dust of the earth; so that if a man could number the dust of the earth, then your descendants also could be numbered. Arise, walk in the land through its length and its width, for I give it to you.
>
> Genesis 13:14–17

That is a lot of acreage God was deeding to Abraham, and note that the land was promised not only to Abraham but to his *descendants*. He and Sarah were still childless! And they were not getting any younger. Yet God promised a child "from your own body" as an heir (Genesis 15:4). Directing Abraham's gaze to the night sky, God said, "Look now toward heaven, and count the stars if you are able to number them. . . . So shall your descendants be" (Genesis 15:5).

Imagine the pinpricks of light that covered the velvet blackness of the ancient sky in the days before pollution and electricity obscured the view. Today we know something about the heavens that Abraham never did: Our galaxy, the Milky Way, has about 400 billion stars, give or take a billion.[5] But Abraham was more concerned with faith than astronomy as he pondered God's promise.

Why the stars? What did God want to teach Abraham? The immenseness of the starry sky is a reminder of how small we really are, and God was prompting Abraham to look upward for his strength and supply. Everything Abraham needed would come from heaven, not earth. In fact, Abraham's assignment, like ours, was to bring heaven to earth. All the power, authority and promises of heaven were entrusted to Abraham, and he would never be satisfied with anything less after tasting of the heavenly gift.

The Son of Promise

Yet Abraham was still concerned about his childless state (Genesis 15:2–4). Surely his consternation was heightened with all the talk about descendants like the dust of the earth or the stars of the sky. God's promise had to start with *one* descendant—and that was not happening for Abraham and Sarah. Abraham had prepared to name his closest servant as his heir, but God again promised the impossible: Assuring him that he would have a child of his own, this time God formalized His Word with a covenant, accompanied by a rite of sacrifice—foreshadowing Abraham's descendants' relationship with God in the future—and yet another reminder that God had given Abraham and his heirs the land. Although Abraham already had the "deed," so to speak, this time God included the boundary lines: "from the river of Egypt to the great river, the River Euphrates" (verse 18).

But that did not change the fact that ten years after leaving their Mesopotamian home, Abraham and Sarah were still childless. At that point they took matters into their own hands: At Sarah's urging, Abraham sired a child through Sarah's handmaid, Hagar. The result was a boy God named Ishmael, who immediately brought tension and strife into the household. Even before his birth, God told Hagar what to expect: "He shall be a wild man; his hand shall be against every man, and every man's hand against him. And he shall dwell in the presence of all his brethren" (Genesis 16:12).

Abraham loved Ishmael, and he made a bold suggestion to God: "Oh, that Ishmael might live before You!" (Genesis 17:18). Could not *he* just be the son of promise? Even then God held firm to His original plan, clarifying that it was Sarah who would bear Abraham a son to be the recipient of God's everlasting covenant (verse 19).

Surely Abraham was disappointed and perhaps more than a little concerned that time was running out for Sarah and him. The writer of Hebrews tells us it was by faith that Abraham dwelt in the land of promise as in a foreign country. He never considered this earth his home; he was captivated by a city whose builder and maker was God (see Hebrews 11:9–10). Yet every time he looked to the heavens, he must have been reminded of God's many visits and promises. Years passed and the promise remained strong in his heart, but his and Sarah's aging bodies were sending another message. How could they have a child, as old as they were?

It was another thirteen years before God finally announced that it was time. By then Abraham was ninety-nine years old, and Sarah just ten years younger. When she heard the news, she could not suppress laughter at the thought. She and Abraham needed to be reminded, as Mary would centuries later, that nothing is impossible for God (Genesis 18:14; Luke 1:37). A year later, when Sarah was rocking the cradle, her own faith was renewed, and she, too, is listed among the faithful in Hebrews 11 (verse 11).

Blessings, Persecutions and Consequences

Little did Abraham know what lay ahead for his descendants, even though God had foretold what would happen. The blessings of God would overflow, as would the hatred of their enemies, resulting in persecution and slavery of the Jewish people. As the people chosen to receive God's Law, preserve the Law and share the Law with the world, they were and are natural targets for those opposed to God's Law. Widespread hatred was instigated by the spirit of lawlessness, originating from the lawless angel Lucifer, who rebelled against God and hates those who live by the standards of God and His Law.

Never has there been a people so blessed and yet so persecuted in the history of mankind. Throughout their history, persecution of the Jews has followed a predicable pattern: from the expulsions of Jews from Israel and Judah by the Assyrians and Babylonians, to the destruction of the Temple in AD 70 by the Roman general Titus, to the expulsions of Jews from Mainz by Henry II of the Holy Roman Empire and from France by King Philip, to the Inquisition in Spain that focused especially on the Jews, to the massacres of Jews in the Ukraine (1648) and Poland (1768), to the first anti-Jewish congress in Dresden, Germany, in 1882, to the millions of Jews killed by the Nazis in the Holocaust, to the expulsion of Jews from Egypt in 1956 and their execution in Iraq in 1969.

Reflecting on the plight of the Jewish people, Mark Twain wrote in 1899,

If the statistics are right, the Jews constitute but one quarter of one percent of the human race. It suggests a nebulous puff of star dust lost in the blaze of the Milky Way. Properly, the Jew ought hardly to be heard of, but he is heard of, has always been heard of. He is as prominent on the planet as any other people, and his importance is extravagantly out of proportion to the smallness of his bulk.

His contributions to the world's list of great names in literature, science, art, music, finance, medicine and abstruse learning are also very out of proportion to the weakness of his numbers. He has made a marvelous fight in this world in all ages; and has done it with his hands tied behind him. He could be vain of himself and be excused for it. The Egyptians, the Babylonians and the Persians rose, filled the planet with sound and splendor, then faded to dream-stuff and passed away; the Greeks and Romans followed and made a vast noise, and they were gone; other people have sprung up and held their torch high for a time but it burned out, and they sit in twilight now, and have vanished.

The Jew saw them all, survived them all, and is now what he always was, exhibiting no decadence, no infirmities of age, no weakening of his parts, no slowing of his energies, no dulling of his alert but aggressive mind. All things are mortal but the Jews; all other forces pass, but he remains. What is the secret of his immortality?[6]

In addition to suffering persecutions, Abraham's heirs have also had to contend with the offspring of Isaac's brother, Ishmael. The conflict that arose between Hagar and Sarah continues to this day, as Ishmael's descendants (the Arab people) contend with the descendants of Sarah's son Isaac (the Jewish people). This does not mean, as some seem to suggest, that one group is all good and the other all bad. God knows each person's heart, and every individual will be judged accordingly. Even so, the tensions between the two groups are not likely to be resolved anytime soon. When God predicted that Ishmael's "hand shall be against every man"

(Genesis 16:12), He was telling Abraham, *There are consequences for what you did, and your descendants will face ramifications you didn't expect. They are not going to tame the descendants of Ishmael, and the result will be constant conflict.*

A Short History of the Land

With the birth of Isaac, Abraham and Sarah—who had lived in the new land more as tourists than residents—finally had not only the deed to the property but someone to pass it on to. They realized it was not their land for just a generation or two; God made it clear that it would be an "everlasting possession" (Genesis 17:8).

I believe this promise to the descendants of Abraham is as valid today as when it was first uttered from the mouth of God. If you believe the Bible is the Word of God and that the promises God made to Abraham are true, then you cannot have another position. All efforts to bring about peace in the Middle East, to bring its peoples together, will be futile. God governs the affairs of humankind, and this truth overrides all other claims.

That does not mean, of course, we should not do everything we can to bring peace to a turbulent world; it simply means that God's prophetic plan will ultimately supersede all human political maneuvering and economic pressure. Israel's situation does not depend on luck or fate. A worldview based on the Bible does not allow that possibility. What God has promised *will* come to pass.

Theologian Wayne Grudem has written,

There is no such thing as "Luck" or "Chance." All things come to pass by God's wise providence. This means that we should adopt a much more "personal" understanding of the universe and the events in it. The universe is not governed by impersonal fate or luck, but by a personal God. Nothing "just happens"—we should see God's hand in events throughout the day, causing all things to work together for good for those who love him.[7]

Just because God said the land belongs to the children of Abraham does not mean the rest of the world will let them have it. In fact, the Hebrew nation has never had full possession of the land up to the boundaries God defined in Genesis 15:18; the closest they have come was during the reign of Solomon, for a short time. The land that the nation of Israel currently occupies is a very small fraction of Abraham's land grant. Today Arabs control 99.9 percent of Middle Eastern lands, leaving Israel less than one tenth of a percent.[8]

In times past, any number of reasons prevented the Israelites from maintaining possession of the land. One of the first such examples was a massive famine during the days of Joseph. You know the story: After Joseph was sold by his brothers as a slave, he rose to become second in command over all Egypt. When famine struck, he arranged for his entire family (seventy people or so) to move to Egypt, where there was ample food. Rather than returning home, however, they stayed. (Life must have been good in Egypt!) Over four centuries they grew into a nation of well over a million people, and their intimidating presence led the Egyptians to enslave them. Of course, that is exactly what God had predicted (Genesis 15:13–16)—but He also promised to deliver His people and return them to their land.

It fell to Moses to lead the people out of Egypt and back to the Promised Land, though their stubborn unwillingness to fight the battles necessary to take it for themselves kept them out for forty more years. Joshua was the one who took them in, and God's power enabled the Israelites to clear out the existing strongholds, defeat the current inhabitants and settle the land. God promised to give them "every place on which the sole of your foot treads

... from the wilderness and Lebanon, from the river, the River Euphrates, even to the Western Sea" (Deuteronomy 11:24; see also Joshua 1:3).

Part of the requirement on the people, though, was to completely clear out the unbelieving nations. When they failed to do so, they endured a lengthy period of time in which one enemy after another moved in and took over the land God had promised Israel. Then came the era of the kings, which began with promise. The tribes began to unite behind a single leader as they had under Moses and Joshua. When God established David ("a man after His own heart") as king, Israel began to be a real power again.

It was David who finally uprooted the residents of Jerusalem, claimed the city for Israel and made it his capital, ever to be known as "the City of David" (2 Samuel 5:9). The site, however, had already held a sacred place in God's prophetic plan for a thousand years. It was the mountaintop where Abraham had been instructed by God to sacrifice his long-awaited son Isaac and offer him as a burnt offering (Genesis 22:1–19). It was also the place that David, repenting of a great sin, built an altar of sacrifice and petitioned God to remove the plague of judgment (see 2 Samuel 24:10–25). Later it became the place where Solomon would erect the Temple and implement the sacrifices required by the Law.

During Solomon's dedication of the Temple, the people began to see exactly how special Jerusalem was in God's plan:

Since the day that I brought My people out of the land of Egypt, I have chosen no city from any tribe of Israel in which to build a house, that My name might be there, nor did I choose any man to be a ruler over My people Israel. Yet I have chosen Jerusalem, that My name may be there, and I have chosen David to be over My people Israel.

2 Chronicles 6:5–6

For now I have chosen and sanctified this house, that My name may be there forever; and My eyes and My heart will be there perpetually.

2 Chronicles 7:16

Yet God also made it clear that whether or not the people continued to enjoy His blessing would be up to them:

But if you turn away and forsake My statutes and My commandments which I have set before you, and go and serve other gods, and worship them, then I will uproot them from My land which I have given them; and this house which I have sanctified for My name I will cast out of My sight, and will make it a proverb and a byword among all peoples.

2 Chronicles 7:19–20

Unfortunately, the spiritual slide began before the end of Solomon's reign, resulting in a divided kingdom ruled, for the most part, by a spiritually bankrupt and self-serving bunch. After a couple of centuries, the northern tribes were conquered and exiled to Assyria in 722 BC; Jerusalem followed in 586 BC, when most of its inhabitants were carried away to Babylon. Thus ended the Israelite presence in the Promised Land.

But not forever. So that His people would not be unduly discouraged, God promised through Jeremiah that the Babylonian captivity would last only seventy years (Jeremiah 25:8–14). In fact, while he languished in prison because King Zedekiah did not appreciate his message of doom, Jeremiah received a peculiar command from God: purchase a nearby field. Signed, sealed and witnessed, the deed was put up for safekeeping (see Jeremiah 32:1–12). Why would anyone in his right mind spend seventeen shekels of silver for a field that would soon be in the possession of the invading Babylonians? God's answer was clear: "Houses and fields and vineyards shall be possessed again in this land" (verse 15).

Still, the loss of their homeland had a sobering effect on the Israelites carried off to Babylon (see Psalm 137). Even after they were able to return and rebuild the city and Temple (to some extent), they were never again the same strong nation. After suffering at the hands of Assyria and Babylon, Israel spent most of the balance of biblical history subject to even stronger Greek, and then Roman, conquerors.

Throughout more recent history, God continued to protect the deed to His land, even when His people were not living in it. The story of one conqueror stands out because of his misguided attempt to use biblical prophecy to boost his own reputation. Suleiman the Magnificent was an Ottoman sultan who was said to rule over as many as thirty million people when the Ottoman Empire reached deep into Europe and the Middle East, controlling much of the Mediterranean.

Legend says that in 1541 Suleiman was told of the writing of Ezekiel concerning the East Gate of the Temple in Jerusalem:

Afterward he brought me to the gate, the gate that faces toward the east. And behold, the glory of the God of Israel came from the way of the east. His voice was like the sound of many waters; and the earth shone with His glory.... Then He brought me back to the outer gate of the sanctuary which faces toward the east, but it was shut. And the LORD said to me, "This gate shall be shut; it shall not be opened, and no man shall enter by it, because the LORD God of Israel has entered by it; therefore it shall be shut. As for the prince, because he is the prince, he may sit in it to eat bread before the LORD; he shall enter by way of the vestibule of the gateway, and go out the same way."

Ezekiel 43:1–2; 44:1–3

101

After hearing that only "the prince" was authorized to enter the Temple through the East Gate, Suleiman announced that *he* would pass through the East Gate the next day to prove that he was more powerful than the Jewish Messiah. That night he woke from a nightmare in which he was passing through the East Gate of the Temple and was struck by lightning. The next day he ordered the gate shut, and it has remained sealed since that day.[9]

Even Napoleon Bonaparte, with all his egotism, had respect for and insight into the importance of the Temple to the Jewish people:

> A story is told that one day Napoleon was walking through the streets of Paris and heard weeping coming from a near-by synagogue. He turned to his assistant and asked, "What is going on in there?" "Today is Tisha B'Av," the assistant said, "and the Jews are mourning the loss of their Temple." Napoleon looked toward the synagogue and said, "If the Jews are still crying after so many hundreds of years, then I am certain the Temple will one day be rebuilt."[10]

That dream looked to be extinguished after World War II. Israel had ceased to be a sovereign state some 2,500 years earlier, and its people scattered all over the world. But though they had been dispersed before, never were they so effectively targeted for extinction as during the war. But all that changed in 1948. Just three years after the war's end God brought the people together and restored to them their nation, the nation of Israel. And it has continued to grow: Around eight hundred thousand people lived in the restored Israel in 1948; today there are more than eight million residents, of which more than six million are Jewish. God certainly did a regathering, did He not? Numerous other nations had come and gone on that plot of land, but the descendants of Abraham never lost the deed. It was their everlasting possession.

Now What?

Jerusalem literally means "city of peace"; yet roughly two thousand years ago the Prince of Peace was subjected to a most violent death in the city of peace. Jesus so angered the religious leaders of His day that they arranged to have Him crucified between two thieves. Little did they know they were fulfilling the prophetic plan of God determined before time, which is why Jesus is called "the Lamb slain from the foundation of the world" (Revelation 13:8). Note how Jerusalem has historically been a place of sacrifice, from Abraham to David to Jesus. Since then, the city has been a place of perpetual conflict.

Israel's reestablishment in the Middle East seems to be timed to correlate with a growing Islamic resurgence. The seed of conflict between the descendants of Isaac and Ishmael has grown into a violent and very visible confrontation between the two. Harvard professor Samuel B. Huntington does not profess to be a Christian, yet his take on the current political and religious tension is telling: "Indigenization has been the order of the day throughout the non-Western world in the 1980s and 1990s. The resurgence of Islam and 're-Islamization' are the central themes in Muslim societies."[11] What the indigenization of Islam means for those of us with a Judeo-Christian perspective is that our Western values will be challenged and are vulnerable to being replaced. For centuries Christianity has remained largely unchallenged by non-Western religions. But in a global community that encourages new ideas and promotes cultural assertiveness, Christianity will be forced to rise to the challenge, both politically and theologically.

Though the radical element is still quite a small percentage of Islam, it is impossible to ignore. Islamic leaders do not tend to mince words. Note the following statements,[12] which, apart from the first, were all delivered in recent decades:

- "I was ordered to fight all men until they say, 'There is no god but Allah.'"—Prophet Muhammad's farewell address, March 632 (I find it interesting that Abraham, the father of the Jewish nation, renounced Allah for the true God while Muhammad, a descendant of Abraham through Ishmael, would embrace Allah, the moon god of Arabia.)

- "We will export our revolution throughout the world . . . until the calls 'There is no god but Allah and Muhammad is the messenger of Allah' are echoed all over the world."—Ayatollah Ruhollah Khomeini, 1979

- "I was ordered to fight the people until they say there is no god but Allah, and his prophet Muhammad."—Osama bin Laden, 2001

- "This religion [Islam] will destroy all other religions through the Islamic Jihad fighters."—Jordanian/Palestinian schoolbook, 1998

Israel's proximity to numerous predominantly Islamic countries makes Israelis a natural target of radical Islam, but the United States is also an object of attack. Judaism and Christianity are both based on the principles found in the Word of God. The founding documents of the United States relied so heavily on the moral and religious teaching of the Christian faith that John Adams said, "Our Constitution was made only for a moral and religious people. It is wholly inadequate to the government of any other."[13] This may be why, in 1979, Iranian leader Ruhollah Khomeini referred to the United States as the "Great Satan" and Israel as the "Little Satan."[14]

Islamic antagonism is too great and the rhetoric too strong for this to be merely a foreign policy issue. It points to a spiritual battle that is taking place around us. The battle will escalate and one day culminate when the man of lawlessness, also known as the Antichrist, is revealed (more on that topic in chapter 7). In a Bible commentary I have that was written in the 1800s, the author wrote, "When you see Israel become a Nation you will know the end is near."[15]

Until then, we would do well to remember the last portion of God's original promise to Abraham: "I will bless those who bless you, and I will curse him who curses you; and in you all the families of the earth shall be blessed" (Genesis 12:3).

I take time on a regular basis to bless those of Jewish descent with the Abrahamic blessing. One time at JFK Airport in New York, I saw a group of Orthodox Jewish men waiting in the security line, and I felt compelled to bless them in the name of the God of Abraham. Still, I wondered how they might react to a complete stranger issuing a blessing.

As I walked in their direction, they glanced at me and then returned to their conversation. "Excuse me," I said. "Could I ask you a favor?" They eyed me a bit suspiciously, but one of the younger men asked, "Yes, what is it?" I explained, "In the Torah, God said to Abraham, 'I will bless those who bless you and curse those who curse you.' I'm a Christian who happens to love the Jewish people, and I would like to bless you in the name of the God of Abraham."

To say that they were shocked would be an understatement! After a moment of awkward silence, the younger man reached out, shook my hand and said, "Thank you." What I did was more than show kindness toward another human being; I evoked a heavenly blessing with a promise. I brought the will of heaven to earth in regard to some members of God's chosen people.

Those men are awaiting their Messiah, and I am waiting for the return of my Savior and King. The East Gate of the Temple is still sealed—not by Suleiman the Magnificent, not by Israel, but by God. Yet one day the Messiah will return and use that entrance

again, fulfilling the prophecies of Ezekiel and giving fresh meaning
to familiar Scripture:

> Lift up your heads, O you gates!
> And be lifted up, you everlasting doors!
> And the King of glory shall come in.
> Who is this King of glory?
> The LORD strong and mighty,
> The LORD mighty in battle.
> Lift up your heads, O you gates!
> Lift up, you everlasting doors!
> And the King of glory shall come in.
> Who is this King of glory?
> The LORD of hosts,
> He is the King of glory.
>
> Psalm 24:7–10

6

Strange Alliances and Shaken Nations

RUBE GOLDBERG was a twentieth-century cartoonist and inventor who is best remembered for his creations of absurdly complex contraptions designed to perform simple tasks. For example, swatting a fly was a fourteen-step process that involved carbolic acid, a slingshot, a baseball bat, a dog, a fish and more. Goldberg is said to be the inspiration (although he was never credited) for the children's board game Mouse Trap.

Goldberg went to extremes, but he also demonstrates the importance of putting things in proper sequence. One action leads to the next, and then the next, and then the next. If any of the numerous steps were not accomplished, the fly would not be swatted, the mouse would not be trapped.

When trying to comprehend and appreciate the significance of biblical prophecy, determining the proper sequence of events becomes essential. The prophets, and Jesus Himself, gave us many clues—specific things to look for to indicate that God deemed the time right for a world-changing major event.

This is, of course, much easier to do in retrospect. While Jesus lived, died and was resurrected, a great many of the Old Testament prophecies were fulfilled (most estimates say more than three hundred). Looking back, we can see event after event in Jesus' life that confirmed what the prophets had written centuries before. But it was far more challenging for Jesus' contemporaries to recognize prophecy being fulfilled *during* those foretold events.

Sometimes we get it right. When the wise men showed up at Herod's palace looking for the newborn King of the Jews, Herod had his scribes consult Scripture. They knew of Micah's prophecy that God's appointed ruler would be born in Bethlehem (Micah 5:2), and the wise men soon discovered firsthand how accurate it was.

Other times we are reluctant to believe what is clearly apparent. For example, early in Jesus' ministry He was in the synagogue and was invited to read from the book of Isaiah. It just so happened that the passage was a Messianic prophecy. When He finished reading, He said, essentially, "This is about Me." The people in attendance did not have the faith to believe that the son of Joseph could possibly be their Messiah, and they even planned to kill Him rather than consider that He might know what He was talking about (Luke 4:16–30).

So even though we can now understand the connection between certain prophecies and the birth, life and ministry of Jesus, it can still be perplexing to make sense of the prophetic passages concerning His second coming. In this chapter we want to look at a few crucial passages—one in much detail—and try to see where they fit in the sequence of end time events.

What's New?

Prophecy related to the end of the world is a fascinating subject that interests almost everyone. The question that I am asked most often is, "What is the next big prophetic event?" The reason that question is so relevant is that we are living in unusual days, prophetic days, in which Bible prophecy can be seen unfolding in the daily media reports.

With the advent of RSS web-feed formats, we are able to receive updated news headlines instantly from around the world. We can learn of a developing story in Asia, Europe or any other place worldwide within minutes of it happening. Never before have we been able to receive so much news and information so quickly and easily. Not only do we keep informed of what is happening around the world, sometimes we cannot help but see a correlation between world events and biblical prophecy.

One headline several years ago caught my eye: "Iraq Suffers as the Euphrates River Dwindles." What captured my attention was the significant role, attested in the article, that the River Euphrates plays in the overall biblical narrative and particularly in biblical prophecy. In reporting the story, the *New York Times* referred to the Euphrates as "a river so crucial to the birth of civilization that the Book of Revelation prophesied it drying up as a sign of the end times."[1] This is what I like to refer to as "ripped from the headlines" news that connects our world with the Bible.

The passage referred to is Revelation 16:12: "Then the sixth angel poured out his bowl on the great river Euphrates, and its water was dried up, so that the way of the kings from the east might be prepared." Who are these kings of the east, and why did the *New York Times* think this event worthwhile to include in a front-page story?

John the apostle had previously written of an army of two hundred million soldiers—the same kings of the east—marching toward Israel and crossing a dried-up Euphrates River (Revelation 9:16). When John wrote Revelation, it would have been staggering to even attempt to imagine an army of that size. It is more than interesting that *Time Magazine* reported in 1965 that China claimed to have an army of 200 million.[2] This is an example of how recent media headlines can help us understand the sequence of events included in the Word of God. In the prophetic timetable, this event will occur at the end of the Great Tribulation at the battle of Armageddon (Revelation 16:16).

I have read that Napoleon once gathered his generals around a map of the world, and one of his key advisors suggested an invasion of China. Napoleon replied, "There lies a sleeping giant. Let him sleep. For when he wakes, he will move the world." As the world approaches the last days before the return of the Lord, I envision the forces of Satan gathered around a map of the Church. One demonic leader suggests an all-out invasion, to which Satan responds, "There lies a sleeping giant. If the Church ever awakes and harnesses its power in the Holy Spirit, it will be totally unstoppable."

The Countdown Begins

We saw in the previous chapter the significance of the nation of Israel throughout history. Jerusalem fell to the Babylonians in 586 BC, after which Israel's people were scattered for more than 2,500 years. What I want to emphasize here is that the rebirth of the nation of Israel was a miracle with great prophetic significance. It is the event that initiated the countdown to the last days on God's prophetic clock. Prior to 1948, making sense of Old Testament prophecy was much more challenging because so much of it depends on Israel's status as a nation. But as soon as that criterion had been fulfilled, other events to come seemed much clearer from a prophetic perspective.

Once Israel became a modern state on May 14, 1948, it quickly established itself as a power. The return of the Jewish people took more than sheer determination and opportunity; it was achieved only by the hand of God. His purpose and timing are exact, and the Jewish people have been drawn back to the land in amazing numbers. One of Israel's first acts after her rebirth as a nation was to establish the Law of Return,[3] an official decree that gave all Jewish people worldwide the right to return and to live in Israel as Israeli citizens. This law was more than a piece of legislation; it was divine providence that fulfilled the prophecies spoken by God's prophets. For example:

> Thus says the Lord GOD: "I will gather you from the peoples, assemble you from the countries where you have been scattered, and I will give you the land of Israel."
>
> Ezekiel 11:17

> Fear not, for I am with you; I will bring your descendants from the east, and gather you from the west; I will say to the north, "Give them up!" and to the south, "Do not keep them back!" Bring My sons from afar, and My daughters from the ends of the earth.
>
> Isaiah 43:5–6

> From beyond the rivers of Ethiopia My worshipers, the daughter of My dispersed ones, shall bring My offering.
>
> Zephaniah 3:10

Zephaniah's mention of Ethiopia is especially interesting because thousands of Ethiopian Jews have been returning to Israel in organized movements. The first wave, known as Operation Moses, included 8,000 Ethiopian Jews transported from the Sudan in 1984. It was followed in 1991 by an airlift known as Operation Solomon that carried another 14,500 Jews from Ethiopia to Israel. Although perceived by the world as humanitarian acts of kindness on the part of Israel, these movements are actually the fulfillment of Zephaniah's prophecy. A *New York Times* report said, "No one knows with any certainty the origins of Ethiopia's Jews, but it is clear that they observe the faith the way it was practiced before the First Temple was destroyed 2,500 years ago."[4]

The prophet Jeremiah revealed that God would also call His people out of what is now the land of Russia:

> "Therefore, behold, the days are coming," says the LORD, "that they shall no longer say, 'As the LORD lives who brought up the children of Israel from the land of Egypt,' but, 'As the LORD lives who brought up and led the descendants of the house of Israel from the north country and from all the countries where I had driven them.' And they shall dwell in their own land."
>
> Jeremiah 23:7–8

As of 1939, an estimated 3,400,000 Jews lived in the European portions of the Soviet Union; today just over 300,000 remain.[5] The emigration of Jews out of Russia began well before the Holocaust, as the assassination of Czar Alexander II in 1881 led to pogroms and persecution against Jews:

> Massive emigration began to other parts of Europe and to countries outside of Europe. This exodus continued until the beginning of World War I. All told, 2,400,000 Jews left Europe during the period 1881–1914. From 1914 to the beginning of World War II, another million Jews emigrated from Europe.[6]

Clearly, God was directing the emigration policies of the twentieth century to fulfill His plan. More than half of Russia's Jews would leave, most of whom sought out a home in the land of Israel. According to Jeremiah, movements like those in Ethiopia and Russia are miraculous acts of God on par with His deliverance of the Israelites from Egyptian bondage in the days of Moses!

Ezekiel saw a vision that illustrated how extreme this reassembling of Israel would be after so long a time. God showed him a valley of old, dried-out bones that represented the nation of Israel and asked him if those bones could live again. From a human perspective, the answer was, "Of course not," but Ezekiel wisely left the answer up to God.

God told Ezekiel to prophesy to the bones, after which they began to clatter back together to form skeletons. As Ezekiel watched, the skeletons were covered with muscle, flesh and skin. They had taken human form again but still were not breathing. So after he had prophesied to the bones, God had Ezekiel "prophesy to the breath." The Hebrew word used here is translated "spirit." This was more than mere breath; this was the impartation of the Holy Spirit. The formerly dried-up bones then became a living, breathing, exceedingly great army. And God's message to His people through Ezekiel was clear:

> Behold, O My people, I will open your graves and cause you to come up from your graves, and bring you into the land of Israel. Then you shall know that I am the LORD, when I have opened your graves, O My people, and brought you up from your graves. I will put My Spirit in you, and you shall live, and I will place you in your own land. Then you shall know that I, the LORD, have spoken it and performed it.
>
> Ezekiel 37:12–14

Prime Minister Benjamin Netanyahu quoted from Ezekiel 37 on the 65th anniversary of the liberation of the Nazi concentration camp at Auschwitz. His speech was important for several reasons, but for our purposes, it is noteworthy as it relates to the prophetic timetable. Here is a portion of what he said (in which he refers to Ezekiel 37:11–12):

The Jewish people rose from ashes and destruction, from a terrible pain that can never be healed. Armed with the Jewish spirit, the justice of man, and the vision of the prophets, we sprouted new branches and grew deep roots. Dry bones became covered with flesh, a spirit filled them, and they lived and stood on their own feet.

As Ezekiel prophesized:

"Then He said unto me: These bones are the whole House of Israel. They say, 'Our bones are dried up, our hope is gone; we are doomed.' Prophesy, therefore, and say to them: Thus said the Lord God: I am going to open your graves and lift you out of your graves, O My people, and bring you to the land of Israel."[7]

Anyone who doubts that God is ultimately in control of human history needs to take a closer look at biblical prophecy.

The establishment of Israel as a modern nation puts a lot of different prophecies into clearer perspective. It was a prerequisite for much that is to follow. It is also a clear signal that God's prophetic clock seems to be ticking down toward the last days. Along with a shifting of the spiritual climate all over the world, we are seeing an acceleration of fulfillment of prophecy as well as an increase in lawlessness. Do not let such things alarm you or cause you to lose faith, because as we witness an increase in evil, we will also see an increase in the work of the Holy Spirit. It is God's timing.

Nations United against Israel

Almost immediately after writing about his vision of the valley of dry bones, Ezekiel shared another message from God revealing a major prophetic event on our current horizon. Ezekiel 38 begins with a prophecy concerning a coalition of nations that are bent on the destruction of the nation of Israel. Ezekiel uses ancient names for these nations, which may sound strange to your ears, but once you identify the modern names, you will instantly recognize them and be able to track their movements.

It is important to keep in mind that national boundaries shift over time. Though we tend to think of names as having a very narrow meaning, correct biblical interpretation sometimes requires a broader number of possibilities. Translation from one language to another is often challenging and more of an art than a science—take the term *Ethiopia*, for example. In the last section, we saw how the Lord orchestrated the migration of Jews from modern-day Ethiopia into Israel in accordance with Zephaniah's prophecy in Zephaniah 3:10. Other biblical and ancient references to Ethiopia can refer to a much larger region spanning from Eritrea to Chad and south to Uganda and Kenya.[8] According to the *Zondervan Pictorial Encyclopedia of the Bible*, "At times the reference to Ethiopia is merely one that implies a country lying as far off as possible."[9] The ancient Greeks were similarly flexible in their use of the term: "The ancient Greeks also used 'Ethiopia' to signal other unknown or quasi-mythical lands located to the south or east of the Mediterranean. As a result, even parts of India came to be regarded as 'Ethiopia' in some accounts."[10] In most cases, we will need to study the context and supporting Scriptures to understand the exact location.

One of my goals is to equip you to see what God is doing in the world in our time. You will begin to see the connections, and you will grow in confidence that God is working out all things for His glory and your good. You will also grow in your understanding that God is sovereign and does indeed rule over all of heaven and earth. So first we will take a look at Ezekiel's prophecy, and then we will try to update the names and places he identifies.

Now the word of the LORD came to me, saying, "Son of man, set your face against Gog, of the land of Magog, the prince of Rosh,

Meshech, and Tubal, and prophesy against him, and say, 'Thus says the Lord GOD: "Behold, I am against you, O Gog, the prince of Rosh, Meshech, and Tubal."'"

Ezekiel 38:1–3

God is very specific about the nations that will come against Israel and seek her destruction. Ezekiel begins with Gog and Magog, the prince of Rosh, Meshech and Tubal. These are all references to a single nation, but they highlight different aspects of that nation.

Gog is a title for the leader of *Magog*, a nation named after a grandson of Noah (one of the sons of Japheth—see Genesis 10:2). Various sources confirm that this is the modern state of Russia. Biblically, Magog is described as being north of Israel (Ezekiel 38:15). Josephus associated the Magogites with the Scythians,[11] who resided in what is modern-day Crimea, European Russia and Ukraine. A more recent scholar tells us that Magog

> appears as a country or people of which Gog was the prince. The notices of Magog would lead us to fix a northern locality: it is expressly stated by Ezekiel that "he was to come up from the sides of the north," (Ezekiel 39:2) from a country adjacent to that of Togarmah or Armenia.[12]

Meshech and *Tubal* were also sons of Japheth, brothers of the original Magog. *Rosh*, according to biblical scholar Arno C. Gaebelein, is another reference to the modern state of Russia:

> Careful research has established the fact that the progenitor of Rosh was Tiraz (Gen. x:2) and that Rosh is Russia. All students of Prophecy are agreed that this is the correct meaning of Rosh. The prince of Rosh, means, therefore, the prince or king of the Russian empire.[13]

It is fascinating to realize that God prompted Ezekiel to prophesy nearly two thousand years before Russia (as we know it) became a nation. How could Ezekiel envision a nation with such great strength and power and a coalition so vast? The only answer is by the Spirit of God. Prophecy serves as one of the great proofs of the authority of Scripture.

God's instruction to Ezekiel was clear:

> Prophesy against him, and say, "Thus says the Lord GOD: 'Behold, I am against you, O Gog, the prince of Rosh, Meshech, and Tubal. I will turn you around, put hooks into your jaws, and lead you out, with all your army, horses, and horsemen, all splendidly clothed, a great company with bucklers and shields, all of them handling swords. Persia, Ethiopia, and Libya are with them, all of them with shield and helmet; Gomer and all its troops; the house of Togarmah from the far north and all its troops—many people are with you.'"
>
> Ezekiel 38:2–6

Let's take a look at the other nations that join with Russia in this coming battle. *Persia* is the ancient name for Iran. An Iranian professor explains the name change:

> The suggestion for the change is said to have come from the Iranian ambassador to Germany, who came under the influence of the Nazis. At the time Germany was in the grip of racial fever and cultivated good relations with nations of "Aryan" blood. It is said that some German friends of the ambassador persuaded him that, as with the advent of Reza Shah, Persia had turned a new leaf in its history . . . it was only fitting that the country be called by its own name, "Iran." This would not only signal a new beginning and bring home to the world the new era in Iranian history, but would also signify the Aryan race of its population, as "Iran" is a cognate of "Aryan" and derived from it.[14]

Ethiopia (or *Libya*), often referred to in Scripture as Cush, is not the Ethiopia of Africa but of Arabia. John Hagee explains the connection between Ethiopia and Libya and points to their alliance against Israel:

> There were also states adjacent to Persia that were known as Ethiopia and Libya. When Moses fled from Egypt because he had killed the Egyptian, he went into the wilderness, and there he married an Ethiopian. He did not go south into African Ethiopia, but went into the Ethiopia of the Arabian Peninsula where he married an Ethiopian who was a Shemite. Therefore, when Ezekiel speaks of Persia, Ethiopia, and Libya, he is speaking of the Arab states.[15]

Gomer is considered by most scholars to be a reference to Germany. The late Dr. Charles Lee Feinberg, professor of Semitics and Old Testament at Dallas Theological Seminary and Talbot Theological Seminary (now Talbot School of Theology), wrote that Gomer was the "hordes of the Cimmerians, tribes that settled along the Danube and Rhine and later formed the Germanic people."[16] Like the United States, Germany has recently experienced its share of lawlessness, bringing a measure of fear to its population. In the summer of 2016, it was reported that German officials planned to tell citizens to stockpile food and water in the event of an attack or other catastrophe. While they do not foresee a national attack on German soil, recent Islamist terrorist attacks in Germany have prompted a new sense of concern.[17]

Togarmah is modern-day Turkey. This is a fascinating member of the Russian alliance given Turkey's strategic place in the NATO alliance. Turkey is the only Muslim-majority member in NATO. The website Global Firepower states that Turkey's active and reserve military consists of nearly six hundred thousand troops and ranks 8th of 126 militaries in the world.[18]

The Coming Conflict

After singling out the nations that He told Ezekiel to prophesy against, God explains *why*. Addressing Magog (Russia) and its allies, He says,

> In the latter years you will come into the land of those brought back from the sword and gathered from many people on the mountains of Israel, which had long been desolate; they were brought out of the nations, and now all of them dwell safely. You will ascend, coming like a storm, covering the land like a cloud, you and all your troops and many peoples with you.
>
> Ezekiel 38:8–9

The coalition of northern nations will unite and attack Israel, but their efforts are futile because God is fighting for Israel:

> I will rain down on him, on his troops, and on the many peoples who are with him, flooding rain, great hailstones, fire, and brimstone. Thus I will magnify Myself and sanctify Myself, and I will be known in the eyes of many nations. Then they shall know that I am the LORD.
>
> Ezekiel 38:22–23

Ezekiel's prophecy is fascinating from so many angles. Of particular interest is the coalition of nations that are arrayed against Israel. In her short modern history, Israel has faced some formidable enemies, but never an alliance of this size.

Regarding the sequence of prophetic events, Ezekiel makes it clear that two requirements must be met before this battle can unfold. First, the people Israel will be back in their own land, a miraculous regathering that took place in 1948. The second requirement is that the attack will take place "in the latter years" (verse 8). This could have indicated that the event would not be fulfilled in Ezekiel's lifetime, but here the term used for "latter years" dates this prophecy to the last days before the return of Christ.

Still, this united front opposing Israel takes place prior to the previously mentioned events of the Tribulation (the drying of the Euphrates River, the march of the kings of the east and the battle of Armageddon). In fact, once the names of the ancient nations are updated to their modern-day equivalents, both religious and secular observers see Ezekiel's prophecy taking place today. Let's look at just a few of their comments:

> Ezekiel's roster of nations for the Gog-Magog war continues to align perfectly for the first time in history. "Persia, Ethiopia, and Libya with them;... Gomer, and all his bands; the house of Togarmah of the north quarters, and all his bands: and many people with thee." The other nations on Ezekiel's roster are all either Russian client states or old Soviet client states, with the exception of Turkey, which is rapidly being pushed back into the Islamic world by the European Union.
>
> Darrell G. Young of Focus on Jerusalem[19]

> In the post-Soviet period, Tehran and Moscow began to view and term their cooperation as "strategic"—each side viewing the other as integral to its own national security, internal stability, and territorial integrity.
>
> Brenda Shaffer of the Washington Institute
> for Near East Policy[20]

> Iran has been around for the last [7 to] 10 thousand years. They (the Israelis) have been occupying those territories for the last 60 to 70 years, with the support and force of the Westerners. They have no roots there in history.... We don't even count them as

any part of any equation for Iran. During a historical phase, they [the Israelis] represent minimal disturbances that come into the picture and are then eliminated.

Iranian President Mahmoud Ahmadinejad[21]

Turkey warns it could leave NATO because of a "lack of support by the West" as the country forms close ties with Russia.

August 10, 2016, headline in the *Daily Mail*[22]

The tension between Israel and all these nations is more than a clash of ideas. A close examination of each of these nations will demonstrate one thing they have in common: a significant Islamic population. In Iran, Sudan, Libya and Turkey, Islam is, if not the official religion, the dominant one, as the vast majority of residents—as high as 98 percent—consider themselves Muslim.

In his seminal work, Harvard scholar Samuel P. Huntington refers to the Islamic resurgence as "a broad intellectual, cultural, social and political movement prevalent throughout the Islamic world."[23] Huntington was also cited in a *Washington Times* opinion article to rebut current casual attitudes toward Islam. Shortly after the November 2015 terrorist attacks in Paris, Robert W. Merry criticized President Obama's statement that the attack was not just against Paris or the French people but "on all of humanity and the universal values that we share":

This is dangerously wrongheaded. History is not about all of humanity struggling to preserve and protect universal values against benighted peoples here and there who operate outside the confines of those shared values. History is about distinct civilizations and cultures that struggle to define themselves and maintain their identities in the face of ongoing threats and challenges from other civilizations and cultures.

121

Compare the president's gauzy notion to what the late Samuel P. Huntington, probably the greatest political scientist of his generation, had to say about the relationship between the West and Islam. "Some Westerners," wrote Huntington, "have argued that the West does not have problems with Islam but only with violent Islamist extremists. Fourteen hundred years of history demonstrate otherwise."[24]

As the events of Ezekiel's prophecy start to occur and a number of powerful nations begin to align themselves against Israel, the situation might appear grim and threatening; but we have not seen Ezekiel's entire message yet. The coalition of earthly powers thinks they are behind this attack, but God has planned every aspect of it. God tells Israel's enemies (through Ezekiel), "I will turn you around, put hooks into your jaws, and lead you out, with all your army, horses, and horsemen, all splendidly clothed, a great company with bucklers and shields, all of them handling swords" (Ezekiel 38:4).

What is the "hook" that God will use to draw the armies of Gog and Magog into this battle? Some have speculated it will be the vast oil and gas reserves of Israel, or perhaps Russia's desire to regain its status as a superpower. One thing is certain: This is a battle that God has arranged to order His divine plan for the end of the ages. Nothing will appease or deter this army.

Even though Israel's enemies "will ascend, coming like a storm, covering the land like a cloud" and "will make an evil plan" (verses 9–10), God is all-powerful. He arranges all things for His glory and to achieve His divine end. He is never random or absent from His creation. When He acts, He acts with the end in mind. God informs Ezekiel that this will occur in the "latter days" and that it will achieve a divine purpose: "so that the nations may know Me" (verse 16).

God will superintend these enemies of Israel in much the same way He did the defiant Pharaoh, who never intended to let the ancient Israelites leave Egypt: "For the Scripture says to the Pharaoh, 'For this very purpose I have raised you up, that I may show My power in you, and that My name may be declared in all the earth'" (Romans 9:17). God arranges and directs all the people and events of the earth in order to move humankind toward His desired end. Paul reminds us that God "works all things according to the counsel of His will" (Ephesians 1:11). This truth brings comfort, especially in times of difficulty and confusion. We can be assured that God is in control and "that all things work together for good to those who love God, to those who are the called according to His purpose" (Romans 8:28).

Ezekiel continues to reveal God's heart for Israel and His plan for Gog:

> "And it will come to pass at the same time, when Gog comes against the land of Israel," says the Lord GOD, "that My fury will show in My face. For in My jealousy and in the fire of My wrath I have spoken: 'Surely in that day there shall be a great earthquake in the land of Israel, so that the fish of the sea, the birds of the heavens, the beasts of the field, all creeping things that creep on the earth, and all men who are on the face of the earth shall shake at My presence. The mountains shall be thrown down, the steep places shall fall, and every wall shall fall to the ground.'"
>
> Ezekiel 38:18–20

What immediately caught my attention in this passage is the effect of the earthquake. When the Bible says that every wall shall fall to the ground, it means *every* wall. The reason this is significant is that the Dome of the Rock and the Al-Aqsa mosque, two very significant religious sites in Islam, rest on the Temple Mount. This passage could hold the key to the rebuilding of the Jewish Temple in Jerusalem and the entrance of the Antichrist to establish a covenant with Israel (Daniel 9:27). The earthquake and judgment described in Ezekiel 38:18–20 are not ordinary but supernatural.

For a while the scene is horrific for Israel. The invading armies "will ascend, coming like a storm, covering the land like a cloud" (verse 9). The air is filled with dust from the boots of an army that can only be described as a coming storm that covers the land. Like a scene from *The Lord of the Rings*, the width and depth of the army is beyond comprehension. They are confident and defiant against the God of Israel.

Then, without warning, God begins to rain down His wrath on the armies of Gog and Magog. God calls for a sword, and first the soldiers turn on one another (verse 21). Then begins a "flooding rain, great hailstones, fire, and brimstone" (verse 22). The aggressors ultimately learn that Israel's God is in total control. God says, "Thus I will magnify Myself and sanctify Myself, and I will be known in the eyes of many nations. Then they shall know that I am the LORD" (verse 23).

Ezekiel's prophecy continues in Ezekiel 39, foreseeing the total defeat of the armies of Gog and Magog. In fact, he says it will take seven months to bury the dead and purify the land again after that conflict (Ezekiel 39:12). And the enemy weapons that are collected will provide enough fuel for fires to last seven years (verses 9–10). There will be no doubt who is responsible for the ultimate victory: "Then they shall know that I am the LORD. So I will make My holy name known in the midst of My people Israel, and I will not let them profane My holy name anymore. Then the nations shall know that I am the LORD, the Holy One in Israel" (verses 6–7).

Even Worse Days to Come

We have spent most of this chapter looking at Ezekiel's prophecies about the "latter days." With such a graphic depiction of massive armies, Israel as a target and God raining hailstones to achieve a great and unexpected victory, it might be natural to presume Ezekiel is describing Armageddon (Revelation 16:16). That is not the case, however.

While there are many parallels between Ezekiel's vision of the battle and John's vision of Armageddon in Revelation, some significant differences make it clear that Scripture is describing different battles. The battle in Ezekiel is distinct and is on the horizon. The result of this initial conflict will be a massive upheaval of civilized society that destabilizes the balance of power in the Middle East. Out of the chaos and crisis will arise someone with an effective plan of recovery, promising (and providing) peace. But once he is in control, this supposed man of peace will turn out to be the man of lawlessness (see 2 Thessalonians 2:3–4)—better known as the Antichrist. The next chapter will focus on this satanic figure.

In the meantime, we will continue to see a rise in lawlessness as the turmoil in the Middle East escalates. World leaders will continue to pontificate about their progress in the region, but all their talk will be to no avail. What was once isolated and random will become more common and strategic. What society fails to understand is that the motive behind lawlessness is to create chaos and disorder on a global scale.

Ezekiel was by no means the only prophet who saw the coming problems that Israel will face, which will subsequently affect the rest of the world. Haggai wrote of a literal shakeup in the latter days:

For thus says the LORD of hosts: "Once more (it is a little while) I will shake heaven and earth, the sea and dry land; and I will shake all nations, and they shall come to the Desire of All Nations, and I will fill this temple with glory," says the Lord of hosts.

Haggai 2:6–7

The conflict between good and evil has been ongoing since the Garden, and it will become worse as the heavenly struggle results in greater shaking of the human realm in regard to relationships, government and economics. The scene will be set for a "hero" who promises answers and peace.

The prophet Zechariah said that God would make Jerusalem "a cup of drunkenness to all the surrounding peoples, when they lay siege against Judah and Jerusalem" (Zechariah 12:2). The word that is translated "drunkenness" refers to the reeling motion that occurs when someone is intoxicated. All of the world will be like a drunken man trying to solve a problem that has no answer. The frustration and hatred will finally reach a fevered pitch among the nations. As a result, Jerusalem will become "a very heavy stone for all peoples" (verse 3).

As we look at all these prophecies about difficult times to come, we need to keep reminding ourselves that God has everything timed out and planned, and that He will achieve His purposes for each of us. It should be extremely comforting to realize that He keeps His eye on the culmination of history. Human history as we know it will reach a climax at the Second Coming of Jesus Christ (Revelation 19:11), when the final enemy is judged and the eternal Son of God takes His seat on the throne and establishes His Kingdom on earth.

The book of Proverbs tells us, "The king's heart is in the hand of the Lord, like the rivers of water; He turns it wherever He wishes" (Proverbs 21:1). While it may seem that the world is spinning out of control, the reality is that God is moving people and nations toward a desired end. If we step back and look at the history of humanity, we can see how God has arranged the details of the past and then trust Him to oversee the events of the future.

As "children of God," we are called to avoid sin and lawlessness (1 John 3:1, 4). When we walk in the Spirit and extend the love of God, we honor Him and advance His Kingdom on earth, bringing joy to the Father's heart. Even during these days of increasing lawlessness, we are called to be different. We are to be world changers.

7

The Antichrist:
Man of Lawlessness

IDENTITY THEFT. Phishing. Pyramid schemes. Counterfeit products. Health insurance fraud. Telephone con artists. Electronic skimmers.

Almost every day, it seems, we hear of a new scam to cheat naïve victims out of their money, leaving them angry, embarrassed and in financial straits. Occasionally even established and respectable institutions are fooled by polished and practiced presentations that convince them to invest in a surefire opportunity. Too late they discover it was a well-executed fly-by-night con job, leaving them red-faced as they explain to their customers, clients and stockholders.

One of the reasons such fraudulent schemes flourish is because they play on what people want to hear. "I'm on your side; you can trust me." "Here's a quick and easy way to get rich." "I can save you a lot of time and trouble if you just give me your Social Security number." Schemes based on lies like this have caused a tremendous amount of hardship and pain.

But the world's biggest con artist is yet to come.

Spiritual Identity Theft

In the previous chapter I explained that the next big prophetic event would be the war described in Ezekiel 38–39. When Israel became a nation in 1948, the prophetic clock began to tick, giving rise to a number of other fulfilled prophecies in Scripture, all of which bring us back to the land of Israel. The aftermath of this great battle will leave the world reeling. Nations will scramble to establish new alliances and trade agreements. At the same time the battle will be a catalyst for worldwide economic growth.

The war described by the prophet Ezekiel will send shockwaves around the world, and as the world experiences more instability, the danger of deception will increase exponentially. The apostle Paul warned his Thessalonian readers to expect a "falling away" from the faith (2 Thessalonians 2:3). The Greek word for "falling away" is *apostasía*, from which we derive our English word *apostasy*. Paul's message to Timothy was similar: "In latter times some will depart from the faith, giving heed to deceiving spirits and doctrines of demons" (1 Timothy 4:1).

This increasing apostasy will culminate in the rise of a powerful figure who, as we will see, is known by several titles. Once the foundation of lawlessness is laid and apostasy reaches a climax, this figure will appear not as an evil, despotic ruler but a winsome, world-class leader who promises peace. He is a con man *par excellence*, but we can piece together his true nature by examining his names and key references to him throughout Scripture.

Antichrist—Even though the word *Antichrist* appears only five times in the Bible (1 John 2:18 [twice], 2:22; 4:3; and 2 John 1:7), this has become the most common title for the captivating figure who will appear in the last days. When the word begins with a lower case *a*, it refers in a general sense to anyone who is opposed to Jesus and the Kingdom of God. In other cases the first letter is capitalized, referring to one specific leader—*the* Antichrist—who will arise to personify the spirit of lawlessness and defiance toward God.

Man of sin (2 Thessalonians 2:3)—This is how Paul refers to the Antichrist in the context of the increase in apostasy and lawlessness. The title reveals the Antichrist's true nature as evil, bent on sin and destruction. As an example, Paul says that this person "opposes and exalts himself above all that is called God or that is worshiped, so that he sits as God in the temple of God, showing himself that he is God" (verse 4). He will go to any length to achieve his aim of world domination.

Son of perdition—The term "son of perdition" is the most intriguing of all the names we find to describe the Antichrist. The Greek word for perdition is *apóleia*, which means "destroying" or "waste." This term is used to describe two individuals in the Bible: Judas Iscariot and the Antichrist. In reference to the Antichrist, Paul pairs this term with "man of sin" in 2 Thessalonians 2:3 for added emphasis. Jesus referred to Judas as "the son of perdition" in John 17:12. We know that at some point Satan entered into Judas (see Luke 22:3; John 13:27), and Jesus was fully aware of it: "'Did I not choose you, the twelve, and one of you is a devil?' He spoke of Judas Iscariot, the son of Simon, for it was he who would betray Him, being one of the twelve" (John 6:70–71). (Some people believe that the Antichrist will be Judas Iscariot resurrected.)

The beast—The Antichrist is called "the beast" throughout the book of Revelation (11:7; 13:1–10; 17:7–8; 19:19–20). He receives his power from Satan himself. When the time arrives for his true nature to be revealed, he is shown to be treacherous and unusual in many ways: "The beast that you saw was, and is not, and will ascend out of the bottomless pit and go to perdition" (Revelation 17:8). No one can miss the power this figure wields. To begin with, he will shock and amaze the world after he recovers from what appears to be a fatal wound to the head (Revelation 13:3); his influence just grows from there:

> He performs great signs, so that he even makes fire come down from heaven on the earth in the sight of men. . . . He causes all, both small and great, rich and poor, free and slave, to receive a mark on their right hand or on their foreheads, and that no one may buy or sell except one who has the mark or the name of the beast, or the number of his name. Here is wisdom. Let him who has understanding calculate the number of the beast, for it is the number of a man: His number is 666.
>
> Revelation 13:13, 16–18

The Rapture and Its Effect

You might wonder how the world could be so fooled by this imposter. The truth is that countless people will have been held under a cloak of darkness all along. The Gospel of Jesus Christ is the good news that Jesus died for our sins, was buried and rose from the dead to give us the gift of salvation. When we receive Christ, we receive the Holy Spirit and become able to see and understand spiritual things. But those without Christ cannot see these clear truths; for them, the Gospel is "veiled to those who are perishing, whose minds the god of this age has blinded, who do not believe, lest the light of the gospel of the glory of Christ, who is the image of God, should shine on them" (2 Corinthians 4:3–4).

What would happen if God's Church of born-again, Spirit-filled believers was no longer around to combat the growing lawlessness of those to whom the truth remains veiled? That is the significance of an event commonly referred to as the Rapture:

> For the Lord Himself will descend from heaven with a shout, with the voice of an archangel, and with the trumpet of God. And the dead in Christ will rise first. Then we who are alive and remain shall be caught up together with them in the clouds to meet the Lord in the air. And thus we shall always be with the Lord.
>
> 1 Thessalonians 4:16–17

The phrase "caught up" is the translation of the Greek word *harpázo*, which literally means "to take by force." (We get *rapture* from the Latin word for the same term.) Along with the removal of believers from the earth, the Holy Spirit, who is restraining evil (2 Thessalonians 2:7), will also depart. This helps explain the widespread apostasy and the worldwide acceptance of the Antichrist.

These will be days of foreboding on the face of the earth as the "mystery of lawlessness" (2 Thessalonians 2:7) that began ages ago is now coming to pass. What started with the fall of Lucifer will have intensified and reached a new level:

> The coming of the lawless one is according to the working of Satan, with all power, signs, and lying wonders, and with all unrighteous deception among those who perish, because they did not receive the love of the truth, that they might be saved. And for this reason God will send them strong delusion, that they should believe the lie, that they all may be condemned who did not believe the truth but had pleasure in unrighteousness.
>
> 2 Thessalonians 2:9–12

It may surprise you that it is God who sends the "strong delusion" on the inhabitants of the earth. This is in response to their denial of the truth and rejection of Christ. In place of the truth (John 14:6) they will now believe the lie (2 Thessalonians 2:11). We see a similar action on the part of God in the book of Isaiah: "So will I choose their delusions, and bring their fears on them; because, when I called, no one answered, when I spoke they did not hear; but they did evil before My eyes, and chose that in which I do not delight" (Isaiah 66:4).

French philosopher Blaise Pascal is often misquoted as saying that there is a "God-shaped vacuum" in the heart of every person that cannot be filled by any created thing, but only by God the Creator, made known through Jesus Christ. While that is a close (and more easily remembered) approximation of what he wrote in *Pensées*, his actual quote is more detailed and thought provoking:

> What else does this craving, and this helplessness, proclaim but that there was once in man a true happiness, of which all that now remains is the empty print and trace? This he tries in vain to fill with everything around him, seeking in things that are not there the help he cannot find in those that are, though none can help, since this infinite abyss can be filled only with an infinite and immutable object; in other words by God himself.[1]

People in the last days will be looking for a savior of the world and, having rejected Jesus, will gladly welcome the Antichrist and yield to his authority. They are deceived by identity theft at the highest level. All too soon will the world discover that its newly chosen leader, who promised peace and prosperity, is actually a pawn of Satan, who quickly reverts to his true nature of evil and violence—at a level the world has never before seen.

The influx and acceptance of the demonic into our culture will pave the way for the entrance of this individual so sinister that he will make all the despotic rulers of the past look like amateurs.

While the world is still reeling from the aftermath of the war described by Ezekiel, Satan and his demonic forces are moving to install their man for the hour. For generations Satan has been waiting to empower someone as a puppet whom he can control to rule over the world. He tried to tempt Jesus in the wilderness with his hollow offer of all the kingdoms of the world (Matthew 4:8–9), but Jesus refused to settle for an earthly kingdom when a heavenly one awaited Him.

Already we are seeing an unprecedented wave of lawlessness in Europe, America and around the world. The scope and complexity of terror networks will soon make it impossible for local law officials to monitor and quell the rising tide. The provision for martial law, which suspends individual rights, is stated in the U.S. Constitution, article 1, section 9: "The Privilege of the Writ of Habeas Corpus shall not be suspended, unless when in Cases of Rebellion or Invasion the public Safety may require it." Martial law would suspend the executive, legislative and judicial branches of the government and install the highest-ranking military officer as governor.[2] That position, appointed by the president of the United States, is the chairman of the Joint Chiefs of Staff.

One possible scenario for the unchallenged rise of the Antichrist would be for the president to declare martial law and install a military governor to address the problem of civil unrest and terror. Other countries experiencing the same kind of unrest would follow suit and install military governors. The need for coordinated worldwide effort could give rise to a central command center led by one person, similar to the position that General Dwight D. Eisenhower held during World War II as the Supreme Allied Commander of the Allied Expeditionary Force. From this central command center, a multinational, multidisciplinary force would be directed to ensure that the world was safe and resilient against terrorism. The role of the leader could expand as countries face currency manipulation, border control threats and cyber attacks. If the person in this position were indeed the Antichrist, he would wield such far-reaching power that he could access financial data, disrupt essential services and alter or steal classified information.

In addition to the removal of Christian influence in the world leading to an unfettered spread of lawlessness, there is another reason people might put their unbridled faith in the Antichrist, even after his promise of peace is quickly replaced by violence on a worldwide scale. Some economists believe that there is a connection between war and a good economy.

An article in the *Business Insider* a few years ago took a satirical look at the effect that World War II had on the American economy. The author made a tongue-in-cheek suggestion that the best way to grow the economy was to start another world war; while he was not serious about this suggestion, he argued that global war had unexpected positive results that today's more contained conflicts fail to achieve:

> Most economists believe that massive federal government spending on tanks, uniforms, bullets, and battleships ... finally put to an end the paralyzing 'deflationary trap' that had existed since the Crash of 1929. ... The numbers were indeed staggering. From 1940 to 1944, federal spending shot up more than six times from just $9.5 billion to $72 billion. This increase led to a corresponding $75 billion expansion of US nominal GDP. ... In other words, the war effort caused US GDP to increase close to 75% in just four years! The War also wiped out the country's chronic unemployment problems ... [and] drew women into the workforce in unprecedented numbers, thereby greatly expanding economic output.[3]

It is easy to see how effortlessly and quickly a person could rise to worldwide power with promises of peace and security against the global threat of terror coupled with economic prosperity. Our world seems ripe for the coming of the man of lawlessness.

What Time Is It?

It is rare, if not outright unheard of, for groups to discuss matters of the last days without speculating *when* the events will take place. As soon as Jesus had broached the subject of future events with His apostles, they were already asking Him if now was the time (Acts 1:4–7). He immediately reminded them of something He had already told them, that it was not theirs to know God's timeline (Matthew 24:36). Yet He also cautioned them to keep watch for the signs (Matthew 24:37–44).

The apostle Paul refers to "knowing the time" (Romans 13:11) and acting in an appropriate manner. The Greek word he uses for "time" has a different meaning from our normal concept of passing hours, days and weeks. It refers instead to a specific, God-appointed time.

Two primary words are translated "time" in the Bible. The first is *chrónos*, from which we derive our English word *chronology*, which refers to the passing of time. It is how we mark history and plan our future. The second word is *kairós*, which refers to an appointed time, strategic moments and signs of Jesus' return. We need to be watchful for God-appointed times (*kairós*) within the usual passing of time (*chrónos*).

The Bible is very exact in bringing light to these two terms. When we differentiate between the two, we unlock the deeper meaning of what Scripture is saying. Consider this example of how the two words are used in the context of the days prior to the return of the Lord:

> But concerning the times [*chrónos*] and the seasons [*kairós*], brethren, you have no need that I should write to you. For you yourselves

know perfectly that the day of the Lord [Second Coming of Christ] so comes as a thief in the night. For when they say, "Peace and safety!" then sudden destruction [unexpected, unforeseen] comes upon them, as labor pains upon a pregnant woman. And they shall not escape. But you, brethren, are not in [spiritual] darkness, so that this Day should overtake you as a thief. You are all sons of light and sons of the day. We are not of the night nor of darkness."

1 Thessalonians 5:1–5, insertions mine

There are several important messages in this passage. First, note that *chrónos* and *kairós* are used in tandem. When you know where you are in God's time (*kairós*), you will not be shaken by the passing of time (*chrónos*).

Next, read the passage again, this time focusing on the personal pronouns, which refer to two different groups. The first group is represented with the pronouns *you, yourselves* and *we*, referring to those who have been truly born again. The second group, represented by *they* and *them*, comprises those who do not know the Lord and will fall under the great delusion (2 Thessalonians 2:11).

The secular mind tends to view religion, specifically Christianity, as outdated and unable to contribute to society in meaningful ways. Among the most pronounced evidence of this is the lack of understanding about the future of mankind. In contrast, believers have a realistic understanding of day-to-day life as well as special insight into what is happening at the specific time in which we live. Such special insight is necessary because of the coming Day of the Lord.

These are days that demand that we know the time, awake from our sleep and realize that darkness is advancing. People who lack the ability to understand the times are easily shaken by the turn of world events. They question God and worry about the rise of evil in our day. Those with spiritual discernment and a working knowledge of the Word, however, can stand strong and see God's hand in world events. God wants us to be secure in our faith and able to move in the spirit realm with power and confidence.

After all, the demons seem to be aware of God's timetable, although they do not know the exact date. One time, as Jesus approached two men who were demon possessed, they shouted at Him, "Have you come here to torture us before God's appointed time?" (Matthew 8:29 NLT).

The demonic world has knowledge of who Jesus is and the certainty of their coming judgment. This knowledge causes Satan to increase his activity to prepare the way for the man of lawlessness. The devil is advancing toward an end-time scenario that he still believes he can win. He really has no choice in the matter. There is no redemption for fallen spirits, only judgment. Driven by his evil nature, Satan seeks to bring a path of destruction and despair. "He was a murderer from the beginning, and does not stand in the truth, because there is no truth in him. When he speaks a lie, he speaks from his own resources, for he is a liar and the father of it" (John 8:44).

Worldwide acts of lawlessness seem to be random to the untrained eye, but for those who know how to navigate in the spirit realm and read culture, the picture is crystal clear. These are the last days, so we should expect an escalation of lawlessness. The enemy knows that his time is short, and we should be aware of that fact as well.

Living in a Lawless World

Earlier in the chapter I mentioned Paul's warning of a "falling away" from the faith prior to the return of the Lord (2 Thessalonians 2:3). Let's consider further what that will look like.

People will hold to a form of godliness but deny its power (2 Timothy 3:5). As they depart from a true faith in the living

God, demonic spirits will find an easy entrance into the thi,
and the actions of humankind: "Now the Spirit expressly
that in latter times some will depart from the faith, giving heed
to deceiving spirits and doctrines of demons" (1 Timothy 4:1).

This helps explain how the spread of lawlessness can occur as
quickly as it does and why countless people are blinded to what is
happening in our world. The term for "deceiving spirits" (*plános*) can
also be understood as "roving spirits" or "imposter spirits." The King
James Version translates it as "seducing spirits." As we mentioned in
chapter 4, when the strong man is not bound (Luke 11:21), demonic
spirits are free to roam in places that were previously protected by
strong Spirit-filled believers who faithfully stewarded the presence
of God. As those spirits "roam," they deceive and mislead those who
are not well grounded in the faith. They introduce new "doctrines
of demons" that are not in keeping with the Word of God.

Satan is a false god who infiltrates society on every level. He
masquerades as an "angel of light" (2 Corinthians 11:14) and uses
even what appears to be good to bring people into his sphere of
control. He works behind the scenes to deceive and empower evil
men. Lacking wisdom and understanding, they forge ahead to
deceive others. Without a spiritual compass, logic or wisdom, the
world starts spinning out of control.

As lawlessness increases, people will look for a solution, any
solution, to control society and bring back law and order. This will
lay the groundwork for what is to come at the end of days. People
naturally crave security and will do almost anything to possess it.
This is why we move to what we deem are safer neighborhoods,
install alarm systems and seek ways to protect ourselves. The enemy
will leverage this fear to cause us to give up our freedom and rights
in exchange for feeling safe and protected.

Lawlessness will eventually reach a tipping point at which the
people of the earth will cry out for someone to restore stability

and safety. That intense fear is the opportunity that will allow the lawless one to seize control of the world. He will come "with all power, signs, and lying wonders, and with all unrighteous deception among those who perish" (2 Thessalonians 2:9–10).

His advancement will come quickly and without precedent. It will not be a gradual spread of evil but will strike forward and advance so quickly that mankind will fall into fear and despair.

What does all this mean for God's people . . . those of us who are aware of the bleak outlook for the world and are living in these days of ever-increasing lawlessness?

To begin with, we need to remember that "God has not given us a spirit of fear, but of power and of love and of a sound mind" (2 Timothy 1:7). The Lord provides a spirit of knowledge and understanding from His Word and by His Spirit. As we learn to depend on the Lord, we will discover new levels of confidence and peace, even in the midst of the powerful storms of lawlessness blowing throughout the world.

This is a day of the unfolding of God's divine plan to bring glory to Himself. The movement of the Spirit on earth is ready to be released as never before. We can expect to see the works of the Spirit outpace all of the great miracles of the past. As the prophet said, "'Behold, the days are coming,' says the LORD, 'when the plowman shall overtake the reaper'" (Amos 9:13).

It was said of the sons of Issachar that they "had understanding of the times" and knew what Israel ought to do (1 Chronicles 12:32). We need to possess this kind of wisdom in order to influence culture, stop the spread of evil and advance the Kingdom of God. Our goal should be to use the best tools we have and infiltrate the highest levels of society. We need to combine God-given wisdom, anointing by the Holy Spirit and a good mind as we attempt to honor God and improve the moral climate of society. We need Spirit-filled cultural change agents who can influence those inside and outside the faith community. I like the challenge that Eric Metaxas puts before us: "We, as Christians, need to earn intellectual respectability so that we can have a seat at the table during crucial conversations."[4]

As we move closer to the end of the age, we are reminded that "evil men and impostors will grow worse and worse, deceiving and being deceived" (2 Timothy 3:13). The King James Version of that verse says that "evil men and seducers shall wax worse and worse." The phrase *wax worse* caught my attention; it is not an expression you often hear in our day. In the original Greek the word means "to strike forward," "to make progress" or "to advance." (Think of the moon in its "waxing" phase as opposed to "waning.") It is the same word Paul uses in Romans 13:12 when he says, "The night is *far spent*, the day is at hand. Therefore let us cast off the works of darkness, and let us put on the armor of light" (italics mine). He is saying that the darkness can only advance in the areas where we provide access. The Word is strong and sure, and as we stand against the darkness, God is faithful to dispel it before it overtakes us.

As we expand our understanding of the phrase *wax worse*, we gain deeper insight into what God is trying to tell us. Evil will not be abated by an improved government or increased education. Those options cannot combat the spirit of lawlessness that is waxing worse . . . advancing . . . pressing forward . . . and will increase day by day. Lawlessness is an insidious antichrist spirit that seeks to distort and destroy the work of God in our world. The apostle John reminds us to "test the spirits" and to be alert for "the spirit of the Antichrist, which you have heard was coming, and is now already in the world" (1 John 4:1, 3).

The spirit of antichrist will increase over time as the days lead up to *the* Antichrist, but its spread can be challenged by Spirit-filled believers who are actively engaged in spiritual warfare, prayer and fasting. Fasting, when combined with prayer, is a powerful tool for a Spirit-filled believer. You may recall from chapter 4 that Jesus made it clear that some demons cannot be overcome by prayer alone because certain "kinds" of spirits carry more authority and are resistant to prayer by itself. After His disciples had tried and failed to expel an evil spirit, He told them, "This kind does not go out except by prayer and fasting" (Matthew 17:21). As we acknowledge this reality, we need to step up our spiritual commitment, trust in our all-powerful Lord and Savior and do all we can to dispel the darkness of lawlessness all around us.

That does not mean day-to-day life will be easy. Sometimes the darkness can appear insurmountable. For example, the recent increase of attacks by Islamic terrorists has reached such a pace that we hardly have time to react to one before we encounter yet another.

The inspiration for much of what is happening today can be traced back to Osama bin Laden. He was certainly not the first, nor will he be the last, in a long list of those who seek to control or dominate the world. Yet bin Laden had a clear sense of his mission that many others emulate:

> I am one of the servants of Allah. We do our duty of fighting for the sake of the religion of Allah. It is also our duty to send a call to all the people of the world to enjoy this great light and to embrace Islam and experience the happiness in Islam. Our primary mission is nothing but the furthering of this religion.[5]

Of course, the inspiration behind Islamic terrorist attacks reaches far deeper than Islam or Osama bin Laden. How else can we explain the shockingly high incidence of violence by Islamic terrorists? According to the website The Religion of Peace, which publishes a list of what its authors assert are "incidents of deadly violence that are reasonably determined to have been committed out of religious [Islamic] duty," more than 29,000 deadly attacks have occurred since 9/11.[6] Those numbers defy logic and mere ideology. We have to move beyond traditional Western thinking to understand that the battle we face is a spiritual one. "For we do not wrestle against flesh and blood, but against principalities, against powers, against the rulers of the darkness of this age, against spiritual hosts of wickedness in the heavenly places" (Ephesians 6:12).

We do not know when or how the man of lawlessness will appear. One thing we do know is that he is coming. He will give man religion but not God. He will unify the world, create a one-world currency and perform signs and wonders, but there will be no peace on the earth.

As that day approaches, we can expect an intensifying of lawlessness, yet that is no cause for panic or alarm. When Jesus was trying to prepare His closest friends for the world's most lawless act of all time—the cruel, callous and unwarranted crucifixion of the very Son of God—He encouraged them to hold on to their faith, to keep His commandments and to look ahead to a powerful movement of the Holy Spirit (John 14). Twice He urged them, "Let not your heart be troubled" (John 14:1, 27). That is still the best advice for how to maneuver through these increasingly lawless times.

And to reinforce that advice, the next section of this book will focus on a powerful tool that can get you through the very worst circumstances of life: *hope*.

THE POWER OF HOPE

PEOPLE OFTEN THINK OF BIBLICAL PROPHECY as messages of "doom and gloom"; indeed, many times they have seen disastrous predictions come to pass exactly as prophesied. But what people often fail to see is that God reveals the future not to scare people but to prepare those who are willing to listen. Prophecy alerts us to look for signs. It allows us to prepare for the worst and not be caught unawares. Ultimately, prophecy is one of God's ways of showing us that He is in control. He knows exactly what unpleasant events are about to take place, but He always points

His people beyond the "doom and gloom" to a time of restoration and renewal. Now that we have examined the current problem of lawlessness in section 1 and God's warning of even worse times to come in section 2, we want to finish with a realistic look at what God's people should be doing in the here and now. If we cling to the hope that God perpetually holds out to us, we need not grieve the past, cower in the present or fear the future. Hope provides not only comfort but incredible power as well.

8

Spiritual Warfare

SUPPOSE YOU MOVE INTO A NEW HOUSE—the home of your dreams. You get settled and everything feels just right. Things could not be better. In a year or so, your spouse points out a slight crack or two in one of the walls, but you chalk it up to the age of the home or perhaps a slight shift of the foundation. In a couple of weeks the crack has tripled in size, but you hope for the best . . . that it will not get worse and you will be able to repair the damage when you have a free weekend.

But before you can get around to it, the cracks have widened and multiplied, and you realize the foundation of the house has begun to crumble. Too late, you acknowledge that the problem is much more serious than you admitted, and now there is no easy way to deal with it. Your spouse has little empathy when you moan, "How could this happen to us? What are we going to do?"

The signs of problems may be written on the wall (literally!), but human beings tend to ignore what is happening, truly believing that someone somewhere will come up with a simple solution. We need to remember that simple answers to complex questions are most likely wrong. The problems, while they may seem to appear suddenly, have in reality developed over many years.

The world has displayed a number of significant signs of decline in the last several years. Behind complex problems that have developed over time one can find layers of bad decisions, multiple roots and unseen spiritual forces. Like cracks in a wall, many people do not notice or care about such changes . . . until they begin to be personally affected.

The frightening truth is that the foundation of America has not merely shifted; it has cracked, and the house is in danger. We are reminded that "unless the LORD builds the house, they labor in vain who build it; unless the LORD guards the city, the watchman stays awake in vain" (Psalm 127:1). The United States will not recover from its malaise by patching the walls with more dialogue, better education or assigning blame. The problems will only get worse until we begin to repair the foundation. When Americans rightly examine the foundations of our personal lives and that of our nation, we find that we desperately need a fresh movement of God.

A few people saw the cracks developing decades ago. In a speech delivered in 1951, General Douglas MacArthur said,

> In this day of gathering storms, as the moral deterioration of political power spreads its growing infection, it is essential that every spiritual force be mobilized to defend and preserve the religious base upon which this nation was founded. For it is that base which has been the motivating impulse to our moral and national growth. History fails to record a single precedent in which nations subject to moral decay have not passed into political and economic decline. There has been either a spiritual reawakening to overcome the moral lapse, or a progressive deterioration leading to ultimate national disaster.[1]

Just a few years later, Dr. Martin Luther King Jr. reflected on the ills of society in a sermon delivered in February 1954. He recalled how Jesus' parents had to return to Jerusalem after unknowingly leaving Him behind when they headed back to Nazareth after Passover (Luke 2:41–52). Then he concluded, "If we are to go forward, we must go back and rediscover those precious values— that all reality hinges on moral foundations and that all reality has spiritual control."[2]

The Root of the Problem

Well-intentioned people devise all kinds of strategies to correct problems in our nations and our world, but the real battle is spiritual. Principalities and powers seek to control and dominate individuals, communities and even entire nations. Much of the turmoil can be traced back to unrestrained demonic forces operating in the world.

This does not, however, excuse the human element. Humankind has been given the freedom to choose between right and wrong. When we act according to God's Law and establish laws that reflect God's revealed truth, we find that society, while not completely free from turmoil, becomes more orderly and provides a strong deterrent to evil acts. Ultimately the principle of law is derived from God. In society, those who maintain the law are appointed by God to act as His agents for good. A good society allows for the free exchange of ideas, the furtherance of the Gospel and peace among all. The apostle Paul connects authority on earth with authority in heaven when he writes,

> Let every soul be subject to the governing authorities. For there is no authority except from God, and the authorities that exist are appointed by God. Therefore whoever resists the authority resists

the ordinance of God, and those who resist will bring judgment on themselves.

Romans 13:1–2

The kind of lawlessness we see today is perpetrated by those who lack the ability (or the willingness) to look either back or forward, imagining that they will write a better future apart from God. This approach, as we will come to understand, is playing into the hand of the enemy and will open the door for greater acts of lawlessness in our society.

We would do well to remember the words of Aleksandr Solzhenitsyn, who wrote, "From the most ancient times justice has been a two-part concept: virtue triumphs, and vice is punished."[3] Understanding the present and future is critical if we are to survive. Solzhenitsyn also reminds us of an old proverb: "Dwell on the past and you'll lose an eye. Forget the past and you'll lose both eyes."[4]

As we move closer to the end of the age and the return of Christ, we can expect an increase in lawlessness. The reason for this increase, in part, is the unrestrained demonic world; yet as followers of Christ, we do not need to cower on the sidelines and watch evil raise its ugly head. Too often all we see is the problem, forgetting that we are filled with the Spirit of almighty God, who has empowered and commissioned us to bring heaven to earth.

An essential element of spiritual warfare, as in any kind of warfare, is knowing the strategies of your opponent(s). I have found that the technique of the enemy in these last days is threefold: (1) He seeks to isolate us from the power and the presence of God; (2) He wants to diminish the moment in which we live—to distract us from immediate opportunities that God provides; and (3) He wants to polarize us with fear. The enemy operates according to a very deliberate strategy that is uniquely crafted for you. We are warned in Scripture not to be ignorant of his devices (2 Corinthians 2:11).

Remember, you are an end-time warrior who carries the presence of God. As such, you need to be in a community of faith in which you can support and draw strength from one another. Never underestimate what you can do. Never let the enemy convince you that you are worthless or weak. You carry the divine presence of God with you and are mighty in God for the pulling down of spiritual strongholds (2 Corinthians 10:3–6). If we fail to deal with the evil in the world, it will rise to greater heights and destroy the good in all of us.

As in any warfare, courage is required to fight spiritual battles. Ilona Tóth[5] showed the kind of courage in the face of evil that Christians must walk in. Though few in the West have heard of her, she is honored in Hungary for her resistance to Communist rule in the 1950s and is frequently referred to as the Hungarian Joan of Arc. An intelligent student and gifted athlete, Ilona Tóth was finishing her medical degree in 1956 when students in Budapest took to the streets to protest the Soviet-backed political leadership—a protest that turned violent and led to a full-blown revolution. Tóth joined the protesters and later threw her organizational and leadership skills into treating the wounded and running a hospital emergency room during the short war for independence.

It was a losing battle from the start, as Russian strength far surpassed that of the Hungarian townspeople. Yet Ilona saw the Communist threat for what it was: evil. After the war ended, she continued to engage politically against Communism by producing flyers and distributing an underground newspaper. In 1957 she was falsely charged with the murder of a secret policeman and sentenced to death. What did the Communists fear from this 25-year-old woman? They feared the truth. Lawlessness will always try to destroy the voice of truth, and Ilona stood tall for justice and truth. She was standing on a firm foundation. As her desolate mother agonized over Ilona's impending execution, she reportedly consoled her by saying, "Don't cry mother, I will die as a brave Hungarian soldier. You know that the charge is false, and they just want to besmirch the holy revolution." When her mother asked where Christ was, Ilona replied, "Here, right next to me."[6]

Behind the Scenes

We see enough to be aware of some of the spiritual warfare taking place around us on a regular basis, but much goes on that we never comprehend. The book of Daniel reveals some of the conflict that occurs behind the thin veil of this present world. Daniel experienced more than a vision; he experienced an open vision. A vision is a snapshot or picture that reveals something about the present or the future. The person who receives the vision is merely an observer. An open vision, in contrast, includes the person as a participant who takes on an active role. Daniel spoke and felt during the open vision, and he gained understanding from it. Scripture describes numerous visions but far fewer open visions.

Daniel was engaged in such a high level of strategic warfare that he was visited by a figure described as being

> clothed in linen, whose waist was girded with gold . . . His body was like beryl, his face like the appearance of lightning, his eyes like torches of fire, his arms and feet like burnished bronze in color, and the sound of his words like the voice of a multitude.
>
> Daniel 10:5–6

This was no ordinary angel Daniel saw; this was a *theophany*, an appearance of God as a man in the Old Testament. This divine being should be distinguished from both the angel who appears later (verses 10–14) and from Michael (verses 13, 21).

Even though Daniel's companions could not see this heavenly visitor, they heard and sensed that something phenomenal was taking place, and they were so terrified that they ran to hide. Daniel's physical strength was diminished after three weeks of fasting, and he dropped to the floor in a deep sleep. He was awakened by an angel, causing him to tremble on his hands and knees. The angel reassured him of his assignment and then opened even wider his understanding of the Kingdom.

Daniel was operating behind enemy lines, and his bold faith and fasting were disrupting the strongholds of the enemy. Prayer is a powerful weapon, but prayer alone is not always enough. When Jesus' disciples were unable to deliver a demon-possessed boy from an evil spirit, Jesus explained that some of our spiritual battles require both prayer and fasting (Matthew 17:21). Prayer combined with fasting is unstoppable.

The level of the spiritual warfare that surrounded Daniel was heightened because of his assignment for the "latter days" (Daniel 10:14). It was important for God's faithful people to expect and be prepared for a dangerous figure who would appear in these days to come. Daniel described this individual as an arrogant and blasphemous king who exalts himself above all others and seeks to control the world (Daniel 11:36–39). This figure is also identified as the lawless one (2 Thessalonians 2:5–12) and the Antichrist.

The spirit of lawlessness has been present since the fall of Lucifer. Satan has a vast network of demonic forces assigned to cities and regions. The "prince of Persia," for example (Daniel 10:13, 20), was a territorial spirit whose job was to stop or delay the work of God. The angel attending to Daniel had contended with the prince of Persia the entire 21 days Daniel had been fasting, making him unable to respond to Daniel. What is revealed to Daniel here provides information about authority and structure in the Kingdom of God as well as a prophetic glimpse into our future. We see that the angel did not have the authority to defeat the prince of Persia; he needed someone with greater authority.

In the spiritual realm, both angelic and demonic forces have levels of authority. We are told that "Michael, one of the chief princes" (Daniel 10:13) had come to help the angel who was speaking to Daniel. A short time later the angel refers to him as "Michael *your* prince" (verse 21, emphasis mine), indicating that Michael seems to be specifically assigned to the nation of Israel.

In another reference to Michael, in Jude 1:9, "Michael the archangel" is disputing with the devil about the body of Moses, one of the preeminent leaders of the nation of Israel. In the battle over Moses' body, even Michael did not have the authority to rebuke Satan. Michael called on an authority greater than all other; he said, "The Lord rebuke you!" We can gather from this incident that Michael and the devil possess the same authority, or possibly that the devil has greater authority than Michael.

Whenever we engage in spiritual warfare, we need to remember that resistance will increase as the stakes become greater. When Jesus was led into the wilderness to be tempted of the devil, he was operating at the highest level of spiritual warfare. In each of the three temptations, His response was prefaced with the phrase *It is written* (Matthew 4:4, 7, 10). In every case, Jesus appealed to the highest law, the Law of God. Jesus knew the power of the Law to quiet chaos and destroy the works of the enemy. The devil was trying to operate in the realm of lawlessness in all three of the temptations. What is interesting is that he did not deny the Law of God but twisted it for his own benefit. An example of this can be seen in the second temptation: "If You are the Son of God, throw Yourself down. For it is written: 'He shall give His angels charge over you,' and, 'In their hands they shall bear you up, lest you dash your foot against a stone'" (Matthew 4:6).

The devil was crafty in his deceit. He quoted a portion of Scripture that applied to Jesus' identity (Psalm 91:11–12), but he pulled it out of context. The very next verse reads, "You shall tread upon the lion and the cobra, the young lion and the serpent you shall trample underfoot" (verse 13). The reason the devil omitted this portion is because of its prophetic nature. This Scripture, like others, points to the authority and power of the coming Messiah to triumph over evil and destroy the works of the enemy (see Genesis 3:15; 1 John 3:8; Revelation 20:10).

We see from Daniel's account that demonic forces are capable of delaying the answer to prayer, restraining God's angels and frustrating God's people. The interesting thing is that Daniel had been operating according to Kingdom principles. He was humble, fasting, prayerful and expectant. His faith was strong, and his focus was on the one true God. He had every reason to believe that God was going to answer his prayers, so he must have been frustrated when he got no response. Perhaps he wondered if maybe he had done something wrong or suspected that God was not pleased with him, which is a normal reaction to unanswered prayer. In reality, the delay had nothing to do with Daniel, but rather with the battle that was taking place in the spiritual realm. A vast army of unseen spiritual creatures inhabits the world around us. We never know how much activity takes place on a daily basis without our knowledge, but when we encroach into the territory held by the enemy, we can expect to encounter opposition.

The apostle John reveals that the spirit of lawlessness will manifest itself in even greater ways during the last days (1 John 2:18, 22; 4:3). It is a lying spirit that infiltrates the hearts and minds of humankind, causing people to believe a lie rather than understand and embrace the truth. Increasingly, we are living in a self-absorbed society whose people are "lovers of pleasure rather than lovers of God, having a form of godliness but denying its power" (2 Timothy 3:4–5).

As the twentieth century was beginning, a national U.S. magazine asked a number of notable people, "What is the chief danger that confronts us in the new century?" Replies were received from Susan B. Anthony, William Jennings Bryan, Andrew Carnegie, Arthur Conan Doyle and many others. One of the most insightful responses came from William Booth, founder of the Salvation Army:

> In answer to your inquiry, I consider that the chief dangers which confront the coming century will be religion without the Holy Ghost, Christianity without Christ, forgiveness without repentance, salvation without regeneration, politics without God, and heaven without hell.[7]

Suit Up for Spiritual Warfare

As followers of Christ, we are called and equipped to partner with God in the battle for the Kingdom. We are more than simply people who love God and look forward to heaven. Spiritual warfare is taking place all around us, and we are to be spiritual warriors battling for the hearts, minds and souls of men and women. If we were not supposed to participate in the battle, why would God supply us with armor (Ephesians 6:10–18)? Let's look at a few specific actions that will make you a better soldier.

Trust the Power of Prayer

Too often we mistakenly think that prayer is all about us, about meeting our needs. Rather, prayer is a strategic weapon that is crucial in the battle for and the advancement of the Kingdom.

Bill Johnson reminds us of this aspect of prayer: "God has chosen to work through us. We are His delegated authority on planet earth, and prayer is the vehicle that gives occasion for His invasion.

Those who don't pray allow darkness to continue ruling."[8] Did you ever think about prayer like that?

Jesus came to destroy the works of the evil one (1 John 3:8). As Jesus' trusted servants and representatives on earth, we are to oppose the works of darkness and bring the Kingdom message to the world. The more we are in tune with the Holy Spirit, the better equipped we will be to fulfill the mission that we have been given. When we do not pray, we fail to hinder the activity of the enemy and we open the door for lawlessness. Satan is all too eager to advance his cause. Jesus made it clear that Satan "was a murderer from the beginning, and does not stand in the truth, because there is no truth in him. When he speaks a lie, he speaks from his own resources, for he is a liar and the father of it" (John 8:44).

Prayer is such a powerful weapon that the enemy will use all means available to discourage and frustrate you. A key component of prayer is perseverance, especially when you are engaged in high levels of spiritual warfare.

George Müller, who founded an orphanage in Bristol, England, that cared for thousands of orphans in the nineteenth century, was a man who understood the power and importance of prayer. He wrote,

> I live in the spirit of prayer. I pray as I walk about, when I lie down and when I rise up. And the answers are always coming. Thousands and tens of thousands of times have my prayers been answered. When once I am persuaded that a thing is right and for the glory of God, I go on praying for it until the answer comes.[9]

Bind the Strong Man

In scriptural accounts, demonic spirits occupied individuals, cities or regions. They remained because they were not opposed or resisted. I believe that demonic spirits are assigned to geographic regions and cities of the world. These ruling spirits hinder prayer, control government, influence policy, increase crime and interfere with the operation of miracles.

The world was stunned in 1963 when President John F. Kennedy was assassinated in Dallas, Texas. Shaken and alarmed by this act of lawlessness, people asked many questions. Who was behind the murder of an American president? What was the real motive? Few answers were ever satisfying, and we may never know the full truth. We do know, however, that it was a shocking act of lawlessness.

On July 7, 2016, another shocking act was perpetrated in Dallas: a lone gunman shot and killed five police officers during a peaceful protest. Like the Kennedy assassination, this was an evil and murderous action. Like the Kennedy assassination, it was an act of lawlessness. And like the Kennedy assassination, it occurred not just in Dallas but *down the street* from the Dallas County Courthouse. The two ambushes occurred just 0.3 miles from each other. I believe we ought to consider a connection in regard to the spirit realm.

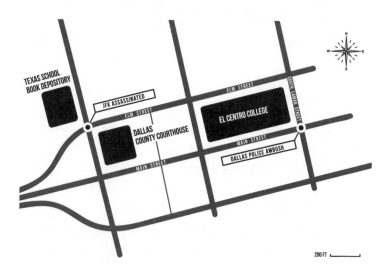

During the 1972 Olympic Games in Munich, West Germany, the Palestinian Black September terrorist group took nine Israeli athletes hostage (after having killed two of their teammates) at the Olympic Village and later murdered them. Next to the Olympic Village, a shopping mall that had been built for the 1972 Olympics became the site of another massacre, when an eighteen-year-old shooter with an illegally obtained Glock pistol opened fire at shoppers and mall employees on July 22, 2016. He killed nine people, two of them as young as thirteen years old, and injured thirty-six others.

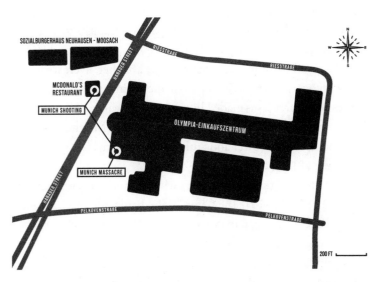

During the ministry of Jesus, He encountered some individuals who were demonized until the evil was confronted and removed. He would "cast out" the spirit, but to where?

In the case of the demon-possessed man of the Gadarenes (Luke 8:26–39), the legion of demons possessing the man recognized Jesus, realized He had authority over them and begged to stay in the region rather than wander aimlessly. They feared being cast into the abyss (verse 31), the place of final confinement (see Revelation 9:1–6). Instead, they pleaded to enter into a herd of swine. When Jesus accommodated their request, the herd immediately ran headlong over the cliff into the water and drowned.

Why did Jesus do as they asked? I believe it was because these were territorial spirits who were assigned a region. One individual was freed from their oppression, yet the entire region needed to acknowledge the power and presence of God (Mark 5:19; Luke 8:39) before the demons could be ousted entirely. Otherwise, the demons would return seven times stronger than before (Matthew 12:43–45).

We saw in chapter 4 that Jesus compared evil spirits to "a strong man, fully armed" who guards what he has accumulated (Luke 11:21–22). His point was that there is another, even stronger, who can overpower the strong man and claim all that was in his possession. Later Jesus made His point even clearer: "All authority has been given to Me in heaven and on earth" (Matthew 28:18). Since Jesus has all power and authority, the enemy is powerless in the name of Jesus.

Jesus empowered His followers with authority over evil spirits (Luke 9:1; 10:17–19). The Church, the Bride of Christ, is called to bind the strong man in every nation, state, city, neighborhood, school and home. Jesus has commissioned us to go in His name, power and authority. We do this through prayer, fasting and seeking to reform laws that allow evil to operate unhindered.

We have been given the "keys of the kingdom of heaven" (Matthew 16:19) for a purpose. It is interesting that Jesus referred to *keys*. The exact number of keys is not stated, yet the plural form suggests that there are multiple doors in the Kingdom.

As I was praying and asking for insight about this, God revealed to me that there are an unlimited number of keys available. With each key comes greater responsibility and authority to make a positive impact in the spiritual realm. In order to overcome the spirit of lawlessness, we are to pursue greater access to Christ's power and authority. Doing so will open doors for revival, healing and miracles that will draw people into a deeper understanding of the character and nature of God. I believe that the *works* of God confirm the *Word* of God. When people see the power of God displayed, they move from skeptic to believer.

Listen for a Word from the Word

Knowledge of the Word of God is essential in spiritual warfare. Two Greek words are translated "word" in the New Testament. The more frequent of the two is *lógos*, used 330 times, primarily in reference to the inspired Word of God. For example, Paul challenges Timothy, "Be diligent to present yourself approved to God, a worker who does not need to be ashamed, rightly dividing the word [*lógos*] of truth" (2 Timothy 2:15). *Lógos* is also used, as in John 1:1, to refer to Jesus: "In the beginning was the Word [*lógos*], and the Word [*lógos*] was with God, and the Word [*lógos*] was God." This is a clear reference to Jesus, the eternal Son of God.

The other Greek word is *rhema*, used about seventy times. The literal translation is "utterance," and it is used primarily to describe insight or revelation from the Word [*lógos*] for a particular situation. I like to say it is a word [*rhema*] from the Word [*lógos*].

When it comes to spiritual warfare and discerning the times, the role of *rhema* becomes critical. Let's look at an example from the temptation of Jesus:

> Then Jesus was led up by the Spirit into the wilderness to be tempted by the devil. And when He had fasted forty days and forty nights, afterward He was hungry. Now when the tempter came to Him, he said, "If You are the Son of God, command that these stones become bread." But He answered and said, "It is written, 'Man shall

not live by bread alone, but by every word [*rhema*] that proceeds from the mouth of God.'"

Matthew 4:1–4

Jesus had been led into the wilderness to be tempted of the devil. His forty-day fast had left Him physically hungry but spiritually alert. During the temptation that appealed to His flesh, He was able to receive the right word for the situation. In that moment of spiritual warfare, the Holy Spirit revealed a word [*rhema*] from the Word [*lógos*] to Jesus from Deuteronomy 8:3. This *rhema* that He recited was not *lógos* randomly selected—it was revealed by the Spirit.

Another example in the context of spiritual warfare is Ephesians 6:17: "And take the helmet of salvation, and the sword of the Spirit, which is the word [*rhema*] of God." Most readers of the Bible do not know Greek and would naturally assume that this passage refers to the written Word of God as being the sword of the Spirit. The distinction is clear, however. In times of intense spiritual warfare we need the Spirit to give us a word [*rhema*] from the Word [*lógos*]. This truth is further amplified by the phrase "the sword of the Spirit." When you engage in conflict with a *rhema*, you have a sword that is able to win the battle. I have found that every time the Lord gives me a *rhema* from His Word, it includes discernment. In other words, you have to know how to apply the *rhema* to your particular situation.

When Victory Comes at Last

In summary, all believers are called to be participants in the spiritual warfare that began with the fall of Lucifer and continues until this day. Someday God will bring the conflict to a decisive and final end, but in the meantime we are called to be vigilant. We need to be faithful in regular prayer and fasting. We need to use our God-given power and authority to "bind the strong man" by opposing and overcoming evil in every way we can. And when we need a clear battle strategy, we must open our spiritual eyes and ears to receive a *rhema* from God—a Spirit-provided word that provides encouragement and direction at just the right time.

It is easy to consider the forces we are up against and quickly become intimidated, if not downright frightened. It is tempting to keep our heads down and try not to make trouble, but that does not accomplish anything. There are no pacifists in spiritual warfare; we are either in the midst of the battle, or we are already defeated. We need to remember Jesus' assurance that even though evil forces are like "a strong man," we have the power of God within us that is far stronger (see 1 John 4:4). And when we stop being reluctant to take a bold stand for God, amazing things can happen.

In chapter 4 I mentioned the revival that occurred in Argentina in 1954, and here I want to provide several more details. When I first read the account of what happened there, I was very intrigued; I was hungry for the works of the Spirit and began to read everything I could find on the subject.

In 1953, a relatively unknown evangelist named Tommy Hicks was invited to Argentina to hold a crusade. His first stop was the palace of the president, Juan Perón, to seek permission to use the football stadium. According to R. Edward Miller, an eyewitness to the revival and author of *Secrets of the Argentine Revival*,

> The guard outside informed him that seeing the president would be impossible. Tommy explained that he was going to hold a salvation-healing crusade. The more Tommy explained, the more interested the guard became. Finally the guard asked, "Do you mean to say that God can heal me?"
>
> "Yes, He can and He will," replied Tommy.

When Tommy laid his hands on the guard, Miller wrote,

> The power of God surged into that guard's body, and in a moment his pain and sickness were gone. . . . Feeling the power of God, the guard was utterly astonished. The guard responded, "You come back tomorrow, and I will get you in to see the President."[10]

Miraculously, Hicks was granted an audience with Perón. Although few people knew it, Perón suffered from such a serious and disfiguring skin disorder that he rarely left the palace. Upon meeting Perón, Hicks laid hands on him, and he was instantly healed of his disease. Perón's healing opened the door for use of the stadium and anything else Hicks might need to accomplish his mission.

One night over dinner, my wife and I were discussing how God had worked in Argentina, and we considered taking a trip to retrace the steps of the revival. I remembered that my good friend Danny Darling was from Argentina, so I texted him to see if he had heard of the revival with Tommy Hicks. He immediately responded that his father-in-law, Juan Carlos Ortiz, had been Hicks's personal secretary during the revival; he even attached a picture from 1954 with Hicks and Ortiz. I could hardly believe how God had arranged this moment—I had no idea Danny's father-in-law had been in the middle of the Argentine revival!

I asked Danny if Juan Carlos Ortiz lived in Buenos Aires, and Danny replied, "No, he lives right here in Orange County." Ortiz has served in ministry since the 1950s as a church planter, professor of theology and author; for a time he was the senior Hispanic pastor at the Crystal Cathedral in Garden Grove, California. Danny and his wife, Vera, arranged for a dinner a few nights later, and for three hours Juan Carlos gave us a firsthand account of the miracles that had accompanied the revival.

According to Juan Carlos, Tommy Hicks had a special anointing to heal that was unlike anything he had seen before. Tommy could not leave the hotel without being mobbed by the crowds who were seeking the power of God to deliver them from various agonizing afflictions. The constant physical, emotional and spiritual drain on Tommy, however, left him exhausted. One day Juan Carlos answered the phone, and the caller insisted on speaking with Tommy. At first Tommy refused the call, but Juan Carlos persuaded him to respond because the caller was in terrible distress. Tommy picked up the phone and said, "In Jesus' name, be healed," and then hung up. Within the hour, the phone rang again. It was the man calling back to report being healed.

Accounts vary as to the size of the crowds and the number of people who came to faith in Christ, but the crowds grew so large that the revival was moved to the Estadio Tomás Adolfo Ducó, home of the Huracán football team, which was the largest available venue. People flocked into the stadium around the clock. It is estimated that during the 54 days of revival, three million people attended and as many as three hundred thousand professed faith in Christ, with a massive number of people being healed.

Dr. R. Edward Miller recounts that the revival began two years prior when "the ruling spirit of Argentina was bound and the strong man of Argentina was overcome."[11] The country was under a spell of darkness and religion. Once the "strong man" was broken, the Spirit was free to move, and move He did!

You will sometimes find yourself in situations that require you to engage in spiritual warfare. When those circumstances come, do not fall into fear or doubt. The enemy will attack your identity and magnify your failures, but never forget that you are handcrafted by God to thrive and make great progress for the Kingdom. Refuse to see the world as others see it. See it from heaven to earth and seize the day that God has given you to bring light to a dark world.

9

How God Deals with Evil

ON DECEMBER 6, 1829, George Wilson and James Porter robbed a United States mail carrier in Pennsylvania. Both men were subsequently captured, tried and, on May 1, 1830, found guilty of robbing the mail and putting the life of the driver in jeopardy. Four weeks later, Wilson and Porter received their sentences: execution by hanging, to be carried out on July 2, 1830.

Before the date of the scheduled execution, some of Wilson's influential friends pleaded for mercy from the president of the United States, Andrew Jackson, on behalf of their colleague. President Jackson issued a formal pardon, but George Wilson refused to accept it!

Wilson's response must have been a first, because the justice system did not know what to do with him. Was he off the hook for what he had done, or not? The case was sent to the U.S. Supreme Court, and Chief Justice John Marshall wrote the opinion:

> A pardon is a deed, to the validity of which delivery is essential, and delivery is not complete without acceptance. It may then be

rejected by the person to whom it is tendered; and if it be rejected, we have discovered no power in a court to force it on him.

In simple terms, a refused pardon was no pardon, so Wilson was sent to the gallows.[1]

As we have said, evil and lawlessness are not new problems; the fact that God has not already put an end to them has caused some people to doubt or desert their faith—and many more feel a sense of deep disappointment. God has always been Creator, King, Judge and Savior. He continues to rule over all and have supreme authority. Because He is holy, righteous and just, we can be certain He will not (and cannot) let sin go unpunished. Yet He is also gracious, loving, merciful and patient, so He has provided a way of rescue for those who place their faith in Him. Jesus Christ bore the consequences of evil on the cross so that we can experience forgiveness, love and the kind of peace only God can provide. Through Jesus, God offers sinful humanity a pardon.

So we have a choice to make. We can be proud like George Wilson, reject an offer of mercy and go to the gallows defiant until the end. Or we can admit we are sinners and accept the mercy of God. In His sovereignty and wisdom, God permits every individual to exercise his or her free will within the boundaries of His divine purpose and redemptive plan for the world. When someone refuses divine mercy, love and power, God allows the continuing downward spiral of individuals and society.

Evil: Whose Fault?

Very few would deny that evil exists and that it wreaks havoc in our world. The reason we need a pardon is that we are by nature drawn to the evil that surrounds us and are easily entangled in it. But who is responsible for the evil and suffering in this world?

In one sense we are all guilty of the unraveling of society. To the extent that we do not do good, we extend the arm of evil and foster injustice in our world. Yet the source of the trouble is not our fellow men but the ancient enemy, Satan, who stands in the shadow of freedom, waiting to hatch his evil trap. So skilled is he in his spiritual guerilla tactics that we rarely acknowledge him as the culprit. He generates all manner of evil but leaves us thinking that evil is an impersonal force that emerges from poverty, greed, ignorance or a myriad of other sources.

From its opening chapters, the Bible confirms that Satan is the personification of evil. He is introduced in the book of Genesis as the serpent who craftily tempted Eve to betray her Creator (Genesis 3:1). Soon afterward, Satan was there to take advantage of Cain's bitterness toward his brother Abel. God intervened and warned Cain to deal with his anger before it escalated into something worse: "Sin lieth at the door. And unto thee shall be *his* desire, and thou shalt rule over *him*" (Genesis 4:7 KJV, emphasis mine). God tried to convince Cain that Satan's desire was to tempt him to do wrong, but that He had provided everything Cain needed to resist the enemy and to rule over him. Cain chose to disregard his position as a son and forfeited his dominion to Satan. This departure from God's design would lead Cain and others into despair and ruin.

We have previously examined how, early in the ministry of Jesus, He was tempted by the devil (Matthew 4:1–11). Here it is important to note that Satan knew all too well that Jesus had come to restore dominion to humankind. Jesus did not face an impersonal force in the wilderness—He faced Satan himself, whose sole agenda was to lead into sin the Son of God. Satan had corrupted the human race, and now he would do the same to Jesus . . . or so he thought. He laid out three tempting opportunities for Jesus to respond to sin that was crouching at the door, but, unlike Cain, Jesus demonstrated dominion over the enemy. The demonstration of authority over Satan and his demonic horde was a lesson that Jesus would pass on to His disciples. They, too, were given the authority and the power to exercise dominion over "the evil one" (Matthew 6:13). Overcoming such challenges would be critical to the success of the advancement of God's Kingdom.

Some people want to blame God for the evil in the world, but this tendency is yet another tactic of the enemy. When Adam and Eve were in the Garden of Eden, the cunning serpent asked Eve, "Has God indeed said, 'You shall not eat of every tree of the garden'?" (Genesis 3:1). His loaded question subtly challenged them to question the goodness of God, suggesting that Eve was being denied the full expression of her freedom. (In other words, "If God were really good, He would let you do what you want to do.") It was similar to what you hear today when people question God's ability or willingness to intervene or stop evil. ("If God were really good, He wouldn't make me endure such unpleasantness.") Dr. Norman L. Geisler writes,

> From a purely apologetic perspective, more skepticism, agnosticism, and atheism have sprung from an inability to answer various aspects of the problem of evil than from any other single issue. What is more, when doubt begins in this area, it moves quickly to other areas.[2]

Regardless how society frames the question or the argument, the blame always seems to rest on a restrictive God who is holding back the best from His children. Harvard professor Michael J. Sandel demonstrates the way humankind approaches freedom from a philosophical perspective:

> Aristotle teaches that justice means giving people what they deserve. And in order to determine who deserves what, we have to determine what virtues are worthy of honor and reward. . . .

By contrast, modern political philosophers—from Immanuel Kant in the eighteenth century to John Rawls in the twentieth century—argue that the principles of justice that define our rights should not rest on any particular conception of virtue, or of the best way to live. Instead, a just society respects each person's freedom to choose his or her own conception of the good life. [3]

Justice??

Even though freedom has been elevated to such a high level, it is nearly impossible to find a situation in which we can eliminate virtue. Modern man is torn between freedom and virtue. Freedom is usually preferred until one person's freedom to choose encroaches on another's individual freedom. When this happens, there is a cry for justice.

Standing against Evil

The questions that arise from the issue of good and evil can keep philosophers debating for centuries: Who is to blame for the bad things that happen in the world? Is it God who restricts our freedom? What if God constrained evil to the point that no one ever acted out the wicked impulses that are within him or her? Better yet, what if no one ever had an evil thought? Would morality exist? Or does morality require a choice? If morality does require a choice, then who or what is sufficient to judge between what is good and what is bad? Can life truly be lived apart from a standard without resulting in chaos, with everyone vying for rights? Do we not need a being (God) higher than humanity to set the standard and then, objectively—without bias—determine the outcome?

Some of the answers are complex, but the simple, foundational truth in the Word of God is that God is good. This attribute of God is not to be relegated behind other, more popular attributes like love, power and wisdom. Its importance can be seen from the very beginning of the biblical narrative, in which God observed that each day of His creation was "good." The culmination of His creative process was humankind, which He said was "very good." A good God creates good things.

The Bible is also clear in establishing that God, along with His Word, is the absolute standard for truth. As the standard-bearer, God alone can determine the basis of justice. In fact, "He has appointed a day on which He will judge the world in righteousness" (Acts 17:31). Until that day, we who are servants of the Most High God must fight the good fight for the Kingdom. Every good and righteous act will further the work of God on earth. Our enemy will not give up ground easily, so we must be determined and consistent in our efforts. John Eadie reminds us that "diplomacy and argument, truce and armistice are of no avail—the keen bright sword of the Spirit must be unsheathed and lifted."[4]

Yale theologian Miroslav Volf is a Croatian who has witnessed the violence of the Balkans. He writes,

> Is it not a bit too arrogant to presume that our contemporary sensibilities about what is compatible with God's love are so much healthier than those of the people of God throughout the whole history of Judaism and Christianity? . . . If God were *not angry* at injustice and deception and *did not* make the final end to violence God would not be worthy of our worship. Here, however, I am less interested in arguing that God's violence is not unworthy of God than in showing that it is beneficial to us.[5]

The awareness that there is a God who acts and judges according to His revealed will is actually a deterrent to evil in our world. One cannot and should not assume the government will ever wield enough power to inhibit crime and the spread of lawlessness apart from God.

In the early 1990s I was invited, along with fifty other pastors, to meet with the first drug czar in the United States, William Bennett. The purpose of the meeting was to lend our support to the war on drugs. Bennett fully believed that the battle was at its roots a moral and spiritual problem that could not be solved apart from God. He said, "Government money cannot instill moral values, but religion can." He added that the struggle was one "of good and evil for the possession of the human soul."[6]

One of the great human values that allows us to move forward with confidence is our hope that one day God will rectify the wrong and establish a new order that is not plagued by violence, sin and injustice. When society loses the fear of God, it breeds fear of another sort—a fear that usually results in appeasement or false hope in humanity. Volf again brings the perspective of someone who has experienced firsthand intense fear and violence:

> My thesis that the practice of nonviolence requires a belief in divine vengeance will be unpopular with many Christians, especially theologians in the West. . . . I suggest imagining that you are delivering a lecture in a war zone (which is where a paper that underlies this chapter was originally delivered). Among your listeners are people whose cities and villages have been first plundered, then burned and leveled to the ground, whose daughters and sisters have been raped, whose fathers and brothers have had their throats slit. The topic of the lecture: a Christian attitude toward violence. The thesis: we should not retaliate since God is perfect noncoercive love. Soon you would discover that it takes the quiet of a suburban home for the birth of the thesis that human nonviolence corresponds to God's refusal to judge. In a scorched land, soaked in the blood of the innocent, it will invariably die.[7]

The Church of Jesus Christ is not powerless against the enemy and the great evil he promotes. On the contrary, the Church has been entrusted with power and authority from on high. In his bestselling book *Destined for the Throne*, author Paul Billheimer confirmed,

> The only force in the world that is contesting Satan's total rule in human affairs is the Church of the living God. . . . If there were nothing to hinder him, Satan would make a hell out of this world here and now. The only saving and healing virtue in the howling deserts of human life flows from the cross of Calvary.[8]

Is the challenge great? Indeed it is. But remember that God intends for us to be warriors in the fiercest battle known to mankind. More than a flesh-and-blood conflict, this is a battle "against principalities, against powers, against the rulers of the darkness of this age, against spiritual hosts of wickedness in the heavenly places" (Ephesians 6:12). It is a spiritual clash that will require that we defend ourselves with "the whole armor of God" (see Ephesians 6:10–18).

This is not a time to grow weary or to let down our guard. It is a time for conquest and victory. It is a time to lift up the banner of the Lord and proclaim the powerful message of the Gospel of Christ Jesus. Too often we live as though spiritual victory depends on our own strength, ability and power, but that is not sufficient if we are to survive in this world, much less thrive. Yet when we are empowered with the Holy Spirit, we invade and exploit the areas of darkness and release those who are held captive.

Ravi Zacharias writes,

> As the face of evil becomes more hideous and ruthless, the face of the future becomes more fearsome and dreaded. Yet for the gospel message this may be the most significant moment in history, for the message of Christ provides the only supernatural hope of a changed heart and life.[9]

Most people who point to the weakness and failure of the Church to affect or change culture never consider that the goodness we *do* find in society is the effect of the Kingdom message. There is no source of goodness other than our good God: "Every good gift and every perfect gift is from above, and comes down from the Father of lights, with whom there is no variation or shadow of turning" (James 1:17). The enemy would love to convince us that our efforts are meaningless, that we have lost the battle and the only thing that remains is to fold our hands and wait for the return of Christ. Reject such thinking and be bold and active in your faith. Jesus knew that fear could short-circuit faith, so He reminded His disciples of their inheritance as sons and daughters of the Father: "Do not fear, little flock, for it is your Father's good pleasure to give you the kingdom" (Luke 12:32).

God has never relied on the majority to accomplish His mission. The power of the Kingdom comes to those who are fully reliant on the Spirit, not to the masses who merely call themselves Christians. It will be the masses who are deceived and lulled into complacency, and already the spirit of the age has had its effect on many. Christianity has become a hobby that is conveniently set aside if something more appealing comes along. I have noticed over the years how many people get serious with God when a crisis occurs, only to fall back into the same complacency when the crisis passes. Maybe those are the ones whom Jesus refers to as being unfit for the Kingdom of God (Luke 9:62).

Mike Bickle, founder of the International House of Prayer in Kansas City, Missouri, characterizes the Day of the Lord in the following manner:

> A theological crisis across the nations will perplex many who will be unable to discern between truth and deception (1 Timothy 4:1–3). Today's hollow programs, prayerlessness, and preaching of a false

gospel of cheap grace in many places will not prepare believers for the coming revival of glory or the encroaching storm of darkness.[10]

As Christ followers, it is essential that we understand our responsibility. We cannot fall back in despair, nor can we give up while we wait for the return of the Lord. As poet and missionary Amy Carmichael stated, "Satan is so much more in earnest than we are—he buys up the opportunity while we are wondering how much it will cost."[11]

We have been given the assignment from God to transform society with the Gospel of Jesus Christ. A clarion call goes out to all who name the name of Christ. Pastor and theologian Dietrich Bonhoeffer understood the cost of following Christ. His opposition to the Nazi regime cost him his life—a life that he willingly gave to stand for truth. He is certainly qualified to ask the question,

> Who stands fast? Only the man whose final standard is not his reason, his principles, his conscience, his freedom, or his virtue, but who is ready to sacrifice all this when he is called to obedient and responsible action in faith and in exclusive allegiance to God—the responsible man, who tries to make his whole life an answer to the question and call of God. Where are these responsible people?[12]

The Magnificent Timing of God

In 1991 my wife, Tammy, and I participated in a mission trip to Oradea, Romania. Our flight pattern took us through Chicago, from where we would fly into Belgrade, Yugoslavia. The timing of our trip was monumental in myriad ways. The Iron Curtain had recently fallen and the Berlin Wall was officially opened. Communist Romanian leader Nicolae Ceaușescu and his wife, Elena, had been found guilty before a military tribunal and executed on

December 25, 1989. Slovenia and Croatia, two of the Yugoslav republics, declared independence on June 25, 1991.

Tammy and I were eager to preach the Gospel in a place that had been under an oppressive government and was closed for decades to the outside world. Christians had endured terrible persecution. Fear of torture and imprisonment would continue for many years. We had heard reports that despite the limited number of Bibles available, the government still considered the importation of Bibles into the country to be an act of smuggling punishable under the law. No matter. We were determined to take Bibles into the country.

We placed as many Bibles as possible in the lining of our suitcases. We did not put a lot of effort into hiding them; any agent who searched our luggage would spot them quickly. We envisioned being arrested and spending the rest of our lives in a Romanian prison, but at the time it seemed like a small price to pay to follow Christ.

When the agent at Chicago's O'Hare International Airport questioned us about the contents of our luggage, we tried to change the subject. He then asked specifically if we had Bibles in our suitcases. I found myself torn between admitting the truth and carrying out our mission. At that moment a supervisor appeared from a doorway, quickly dismissed our agent and took over the interrogation. He waited a moment until the other agent had gone and asked, "You have Bibles in your suitcases, don't you?"

"Yes," I replied.

He said, "I'm going to seal your suitcases all the way to Belgrade. I'm a Christian and will be praying for your work."

When we are faithful to carry out the mission entrusted to us, God is faithful to work out the details. The Lord provided His servant at exactly the right time, confirming that He was with us and intended for us to finish the work we began. This experience deepened our faith and taught us that God, not the government, was ultimately in control. When we are faithful to walk in the Spirit and advance His Kingdom, He is faithful to stop the forces of evil and protect us.

Never be ashamed of the Gospel or doubt its power to transform lives. The Gospel is the power of God unto salvation (Romans 1:16) and the only hope for humankind. Evangelist Reinhard Bonnke reminds us of our strategic role in conquering evil: "Through us God will put an end to evil and to the architect of evil, the devil. Part of that ultimate victory is the present mandate to preach the gospel."[13]

Looking toward a Better Future

In the end, what will be the picture that God paints on the tapestry of humanity? It is a restored and healthy world in which evil has been dealt with and righteousness is exalted to the place of honor it rightly deserves. It is the desire of humankind.

It is comforting and true that we can entrust our future, including judgment, to a faithful God who always does what is good and who never changes. Those who resist the idea of judgment are those who forget that the Judge is the One who died on Calvary for the sins of the world. The Judge is the One who could look, with compassion, into the eyes of the woman caught in adultery and see her potential for life. He also looked into the eyes of her accusers with love, causing them to reconsider *their* authority to judge. He condemned neither. His focus was on wholeness and love. The Judge is the One who healed the sick and never tried to ascribe blame for the sin or shortcomings of the person who was healed.

The restoration of all things is necessary to repair the injustice and suffering of this present age. In the meantime, we long for something better, something that will bridge the gap between how things are and how things should be. C. S. Lewis guides us in this understanding:

> "I reckon," said St Paul, "that the sufferings of this present time are not worthy to be compared with the glory that shall be revealed in us" [Romans 8:18]. If this is so, a book on suffering which says nothing of heaven, is leaving out almost the whole of one side of the account. Scripture and tradition habitually put the joys of heaven into the scale against the sufferings of earth, and no solution of the problem of pain which does not do so can be called a Christian one.[14]

Our Creator designed us with the longing to be whole and free from the hurt and pain that all of creation experiences. One day that desire will become a reality. Consider how God paints the future for humanity:

> The wolf also shall dwell with the lamb, the leopard shall lie down with the young goat, the calf and the young lion and the fatling together; and a little child shall lead them.
>
> Isaiah 11:6

> He shall judge between the nations, and rebuke many people; they shall beat their swords into plowshares, and their spears into pruning hooks; nation shall not lift up sword against nation, neither shall they learn war anymore.
>
> Isaiah 2:4

> For I consider that the sufferings of this present time are not worthy to be compared with the glory which shall be revealed in us. For the earnest expectation of the creation eagerly waits for the revealing of the sons of God. For the creation was subjected to futility, not

willingly, but because of Him who subjected it in hope; because the creation itself also will be delivered from the bondage of corruption into the glorious liberty of the children of God.

Romans 8:18–21

Arise, shine; for your light has come! And the glory of the LORD is risen upon you. For behold, the darkness shall cover the earth, and deep darkness the people; but the LORD will arise over you, and His glory will be seen upon you. The Gentiles shall come to your light, and kings to the brightness of your rising. Lift up your eyes all around, and see: They all gather together, they come to you; your sons shall come from afar, and your daughters shall be nursed at your side. Then you shall see and become radiant, and your heart shall swell with joy; because the abundance of the sea shall be turned to you, the wealth of the Gentiles shall come to you.

Isaiah 60:1–5

Referring to this passage in Isaiah 60, pastor Bill Johnson comments,

Through this prophetic promise God provides specific instruction about our approach to life and what kind of results He is looking for through that approach. We are to live intentionally, knowing the kind of impact we are to have even before we see it for ourselves. The ramifications of this prophetic word go far beyond most of our hopes, dreams, and visions. Isaiah declared entire nations and their leaders would be transformed. We'd then see the wealth of the nations released to the church for kingdom purposes. But all the fruit and breakthrough provided in these promises are connected to one thing—the manifest presence of God upon His people. It's the manifestation of His glory. Herein lies the challenge—we are commanded to arise and shine in the midst of deep, depressing darkness that covers those around us. God responds to our obedience by releasing His glory. Our shining attracts His glory! And it's His glory released that brings about the greatest transformation in lives, cities, and nations.[15]

A Better Outlook

How does God deal with evil? He has many options. In the past He has used a great flood to remove widespread lawlessness and start over with righteous Noah; He has rained fire and brimstone on cities where not even ten righteous people could be found; He has allowed His perpetually defiant people to be carried off into exile by their cruel and powerful enemies. But those and other means were all temporary solutions to a persistent problem that did not go away.

How about today? Those of us who live on this side of the cross have a much more promising outlook. As prevalent as sin and lawlessness seem to be throughout our world, and as distraught as we might be to witness it, we need to remember that *God has already dealt with evil*. The remedy has been provided, the task has been accomplished and the sentence has been passed. All that remains is the execution of the final judgment.

What is keeping God from moving ahead with it? His patience. His love. His grace. His mercy.

People who demand that God quickly provide a final solution for evil may not realize what they are asking. It will be a time "when the Lord Jesus is revealed from heaven with His mighty angels, in flaming fire taking vengeance on those who do not know God" (2 Thessalonians 1:7–8).

Peter was the disciple who often acted without thinking and sometimes lived to regret it. He walked out to Jesus on the water, then panicked and started to sink; he swore to die for Jesus if necessary, but hours later denied Him three times; he went back to fishing after Jesus' resurrection, only to have Jesus put him back on the track of ministry. He must have learned that acting in haste is not usually a good thing. Maybe that is why, as he was reminding his readers that God's judgment is a sure thing and will be sudden and final, he also cautioned them (and us) to be more aware of God's nature:

> Beloved, do not forget this one thing, that with the Lord one day is as a thousand years, and a thousand years as one day. The Lord is not slack concerning His promise, as some count slackness, but is longsuffering toward us, not willing that any should perish but that all should come to repentance.
>
> 2 Peter 3:8–9

God does not want anyone to perish. His pardon is available and accessible to everyone. Every day that God delays judgment is another day the Spirit moves, convicts and calls new believers into the Kingdom. It is another day for the Church to go out into the world and speak boldly about the love of God. Now is the time for action, because most of us have friends or loved ones who, like George Wilson, have rejected God's gracious and magnanimous offer. So far, it is for them as if the pardon never existed. So God, like the father in the Parable of the Prodigal Son, waits. But He will not wait forever. One day, in perfect justice, He will pull the handle on the gallows, pronounce judgment on the devil and his followers and put an end to all evil and lawlessness.

When the Lord is present, miraculous things begin to happen. Results previously thought impossible become possible. Faith in Him brings hope to reality and makes us certain of things we cannot physically see (Hebrews 11:1). I like to say, "You have to see what you cannot see in order to see what you can see." When we begin to move in the supernatural and see what is possible, we open up all the Kingdom possibilities that are awaiting release.

The Church needs to strengthen its faith and resolve now more than ever. As evil and lawlessness spread across the earth, there has never been a time when desperate people have been more in need of a message of hope.

10

Looking Forward with Hope

OUR GOD IS A REWARDER GOD. He is not selfish. He does not like to see us suffer or do without. The enemy would like to make you believe God is not a good God, but the book of Hebrews states what is tried and true: "He is a rewarder of those who diligently seek Him" (Hebrews 11:6). I have found no truth more liberating than this, and I have seen people who lack this understanding suffer lifetimes of frustration, wondering about the character of God.

If someone ever embraces the idea that God's character is somehow flawed, then all sorts of troubling questions follow. *If God is really good, then how can there be suffering in the world? If God is unfair, then why should anyone trust Him?* Such questions illustrate how the enemy infiltrates the minds of humankind. Even the insurance industry refers to a horrible natural disaster as an "act of God."

Have you ever wondered why no one asks the converse of the question? *If God is a bad God, then why is there so much good in the world?* How do you explain the good, the order of the universe and other miracles?

Some years ago a friend of mine was an editor with the *Kansas City Star*. We were discussing the constant barrage of bad news in print and in the media generally. He made a simple but profound statement that resonated with me: The reason the media focus so much on bad news, he said, is their worldview. It was an intriguing statement, and I asked him to elaborate. He said the secular worldview is that people are inherently good, so when they do something bad, it is news.

The Christian worldview of the human condition is just the opposite. The Bible teaches that people are separated from God—sinners. Human nature is bent toward bad and not good. If the news media adopted a Christian worldview, then they would focus more on good news, because good is contrary to human nature.

A. W. Tozer says that when we speak of God as good, we refer to His essential nature:

> Divine goodness, as one of God's attributes, is self-caused, infinite, perfect, and eternal. Since God is immutable, He never varies in intensity of His loving-kindness. He has never been kinder than He is right now, nor will He ever be less kind.[1]

The goodness of God is the foundation of our faith and our expectation. *When we begin with the idea of a God who always does good and who loves us, then our expectation meets our experience.* That simple shift in thinking is remarkably powerful because it realigns us with God's eternal Kingdom. We begin to operate from a perspective of abundance and favor instead of a perspective of poverty and struggle.

Some people embrace a theology that God inflicts evil on people to teach them a lesson or to make them holy. This view usually fails to take into account the consequences of our own bad choices and places undeserved blame on a sovereign and loving God.

God as a Heavenly Father

The perspective that God arranges evil for His children is quite different from what we read in the Bible. Let's look at a couple of passages that illustrate this truth.

In the first passage Jesus speaks of the innate (though imperfect) love and goodness a human father shows toward his children and then contrasts such a level of concern with that of the heavenly Father.

> What man is there among you who, if his son asks for bread, will give him a stone? Or if he asks for a fish, will he give him a serpent? If you then, being evil, know how to give good gifts to your children, how much more will your Father who is in heaven give good things to those who ask Him!
>
> Matthew 7:9–11

If a child is hungry and approaches his father for food, any decent dad will give him what he asks and needs. It would be an act of cruelty to give the child a stone instead of bread, even more so to substitute a serpent if the child asks for fish. The reason this passage on prayer is so important is that it clarifies misconceptions many people have about God's nature. God answers prayer not primarily because we ask but because of His character.

A good God provides the very best for His children. Some people are reluctant to ask for God's favor or blessing in their lives because they believe that would exemplify greed or selfishness. Nothing could be further from the truth. God rejoices when we ask for His blessings. When we ask for His favor, we are essentially saying, "My Father loves me and wants to bless me far more than I could imagine."

During the earthly ministry of Jesus, He encouraged His disciples to expect answers to their prayerful requests: "Until now you have asked nothing in My name. Ask, and you will receive, that your joy may be full" (John 16:24). Paul Billheimer writes,

> God's promises to answer prayer cover such a broad spectrum as to constitute a veritable carte blanche, bearing the authority of His own signature. It is as though God handed us His scepter and begged us to use it, within the constraints of His will.[2]

Another passage to illustrate this principle is the familiar story of the Prodigal Son (Luke 15:11–32). A young man is selfish and wants his inheritance before his father dies so he can leave home and see the world, all at the father's expense. The father, surprisingly, grants his request. Why would any father do this? The key is that this story is not about just any father; it is about the heavenly Father. This act of kindness points to the character of God. It is not a lesson about a wayward son who comes home; it is a story about a benevolent Father. The goodness of the Father can be seen throughout the parable. The son does not understand the depth of his father's love until much later, when he runs out of money and finds himself in a far country, alone and barely surviving. He has developed such a spirit of poverty that he cannot see the goodness of his father. By that time, he perceives himself as a slave and not a son.

> But when he came to himself, he said, "How many of my father's hired servants have bread enough and to spare, and I perish with hunger! I will arise and go to my father, and will say to him, 'Father, I have sinned against heaven and before you, and I am no

longer worthy to be called your son. Make me like one of your hired servants.'"

Luke 15:17–19

The sad truth of the passage is that the Prodigal never saw himself as a son. He did not understand the goodness of his father when he asked for his inheritance, nor does he understand in his despair away from home. He feels guilt and shame, not primarily because of his failure but due to a lack of knowledge about the essential character of the father.

When he returns, he is surprised to discover that the father has been eagerly awaiting him. The father sees him in the distance and runs to love and embrace him. So overwhelming is the father's love that the son cannot find a platform for his confession.

The character of the father dominates the story. He insists, "Bring out the best robe and put it on him, and put a ring on his hand and sandals on his feet. And bring the fatted calf here and kill it, and let us eat and be merry; for this my son was dead and is alive again; he was lost and is found" (verses 22–24).

What kind of father is this? No guilt? No life lessons? This would not be the reaction of many earthly fathers, and the contrast shows the abundant love and goodness of our heavenly Father.

But the story is not over. It continues with the older son, who *also* needs to understand the goodness of the father. When little brother returns from his journey in the far country, the older son is indignant and angry with both the brother and the father. He refuses to join the celebration for the returning Prodigal, even after the father pleads with him. He held the view that many hold today, that the Prodigal did not deserve the kindness of the father. It was not fair! How could the father love, forgive and bless such a clueless and selfish son?

The older son was living with the same poverty of spirit as the Prodigal. In his estimation, *he was good, and now the father was bad*. Only a bad father would show favor to a wayward son. Again we see how a distorted view of the goodness of God can affect our perspective on life.

Yet the father in our story was relentless in his pursuit of the older son. His goodness could be seen on every side. The father patiently waited as the older son expressed his frustration and anger. Once he finished, it was the father's turn to close the discussion with words that ministered love and grace.

The father provided three important truths. The first was *sonship*: "*Son*, you are always with me, and all that I have is yours" (verse 31, emphasis mine).

The older brother had lived under his father's roof for years but never understood that his father was good. He needed to acknowledge that a good father does not show favoritism. He was like many people today who live a life apart from the goodness of God and do not understand sonship. Much of the turmoil in our homes and the world can be directly traced to a lack of understanding that God is good.

The second truth was *relationship*. The father reminded the older brother, "Son, *you are always with me*, and all that I have is yours" (emphasis mine). You might think that after the younger son left home, the older son would be closer to his father, yet he never really knew him. Maybe he made no attempt to know the father because he assumed that he was not worth knowing. We can get so busy working for God that we fail to take the time to get to know the heart of the Father. When we set aside time to abide in His presence, we discover that our Father is much more interested in our relationship *with* Him than our labor *for* Him.

The third truth was that of *inheritance*. The father was incredibly generous: "Son, you are always with me, and *all that I have is yours*" (emphasis mine). All that the father had, he provided for his sons. In his living and his dying, he gave it all that he might further his kingdom. The father knew that future generations would depend on his sons getting a better understanding of his heart. The importance of knowing the goodness of God the Father is essential in every generation, especially those living in the last days who will face unparalleled lawlessness and disregard for Him.

What hope did the younger son have in that far-off country, destitute and detached from his father? What hope did the older son have with his hardened heart that kept him apart from his father just as surely (if not more so) as physical distance? In both cases, their only hope was in a renewed relationship with the father. The younger son realized it, and we can see what a vast difference it made in his life. Jesus ends the story before we see whether or not the older son finally came around. But the parable gives us all hope for the prodigals we know, as well as those we know who are so driven to work for God that they miss the joys of relationship with Him.

Jesus made it clear to His disciples that it was "your Father's good pleasure to give you the kingdom" (Luke 12:32). What a powerful statement! In Christ, we have been adopted into God's family and are partakers of His divine favor. We are "heirs of God and joint heirs with Christ" (Romans 8:17).

As Christ followers, we have been given the authority to carry out the agenda of the Father on earth. With every prayer, we increase in power and advance the Kingdom of God. When we press into the Kingdom, we understand that all the power and provisions of Christ are entrusted to our care. Jesus expects us to carry out the mission of proclaiming the Gospel, healing the sick and advancing the Kingdom.

E. M. Bounds, a Civil War–era attorney and author of numerous books on prayer, taught that God shapes the world by prayer: "The prayers of God's saints are the capital stock in Heaven, by which Christ carries on his great work upon earth."[3]

A Powerful Start

Tammy and I planted Influence Church in Anaheim Hills, California, on February 12, 2012, with a conviction that the works of God would testify to the Word of God. I had been told for much of my ministry that I was a good preacher, but what did that mean? Did it mean that I could communicate well? Was I accomplished in the construction of an outline that could keep everyone awake during the message? What did all that matter if the power of God was not present? Little did I know at the time how God would use our weakness to testify to His strength in an amazing way.

I had read about all the great revivals and longed to be a part of a mighty movement of the Spirit, yet the longing of my heart was not to impress people or to have the largest church. More than anything, I wanted the power of God to be manifest. One of the early moves of God I experienced (a number of years before starting Influence Church) occurred during one hundred days our church devoted to prayer and fasting. I wanted to find a speaker to come during that time who understood the works of the Spirit, so I wrote down the name of every person I could think of who carried some weight in the Christian world and whom I respected.

One day I received a call from a man with a New Zealand accent who identified himself as J. Oswald Sanders. "Pastor," he said, "I've heard of your work and I'd like to come speak at your church. This will be my last trip through the colonies." I thought it was one of my friends playing a joke on me. Who still refers to America as one of the colonies?

Could this really be J. Oswald Sanders? I had cut my teeth on his book *Spiritual Leadership*. Why would the great man of God be calling me? He had served as the director of the China Inland Mission, written forty books and was respected worldwide as a speaker. I politely thanked him for the call and asked if I could have his number and call him back. I waited a couple of days before returning the call. To my utter surprise, it was indeed J. Oswald Sanders.

Sanders's visit was everything I had hoped it would be, and more. A highlight of our time together was discussing great revivals of the past. I commented that I wanted to be a part of a great revival before I died, and I did not care who got it started. He paused for a moment and then replied, "I rather suspect the Holy Spirit will get it started!"

I agreed. "Indeed," I told him, "that is the longing of my heart."

During those hundred days of prayer and fasting, we witnessed many amazing things. A drug dealer walked into my office, confessed his sin and then flushed thousands of dollars' worth of cocaine down the toilet. About midway through the hundred days, I gave an invitation for people to come to Christ, and 157 people flooded the front of the stage in response to the Spirit's moving. Still, I longed for more. I wanted to see an ongoing demonstration of God's presence. I wanted to see people being saved, healed and delivered on a weekly basis. I wanted our church to affect the culture of a community and a city.

When the apostle Paul penned his letter to the church at Corinth, he emphasized this very point:

> For I determined not to know anything among you except Jesus Christ and Him crucified. I was with you in weakness, in fear, and in much trembling. And my speech and my preaching were not with persuasive words of human wisdom, but in demonstration of the Spirit and of power, that your faith should not be in the wisdom of men but in the power of God.
>
> 1 Corinthians 2:2–5

Paul was a learned man and undoubtedly eloquent of speech. He could quote the great teachers of the Law as well as the Greek philosophers who laid claim to the wisdom of the vast Roman Empire. Yet he had come face to face with the risen Lord on the road to Damascus (Acts 9:4–5) and was forever changed. He lost his desire to terrorize the Church as well as for the respect of his Pharisee peers because his life and purpose had been redirected to proclaim the riches of Christ.

Paul came to understand that there is no truth greater than Jesus Christ crucified for our sins. His God encounter humbled and changed him. God was shaping him for an eternal weight of glory that one day would be revealed. This new purpose motivated both his words and his life. The proud, self-righteous, religious Paul would need to yield so that the power of God could be manifest in him. When he recalled speaking with the Corinthians, who took great pride in their learning, he wrote, "My speech and my preaching were not with persuasive words of human wisdom, but in demonstration of the Spirit and of power, that your faith should not be in the wisdom of men but in the power of God" (1 Corinthians 2:4–5). Eloquence yields to the Holy Spirit when the works of the Spirit are manifest, because God's mighty power is seen.

We wanted to establish Influence Church because we realized our world is much like Paul's, in the sense that we have seen and heard religious chatter for years. Week after week, church services provide little more than motivational talks with an occasional mention of Jesus and cleverly contrived ways to draw people back for another week of the same diet.

Even worse, the Church fails to provide a message that is relevant for our day. We hear no shortage of sermons on the environment or discovering the reason for low self-esteem. Where are the revolutionary words of Jesus? We have become soft, offended and uninformed, while the world has become hard, determined and aware. Not so for Paul. He was motivated by a God encounter of the highest order. Paul's humility and hunger made way for the presence of God.

The words that Jesus spoke had come alive for His followers, and the power of the Holy Spirit resided on all who sought Him with a pure heart. They felt a spirit of expectancy that God would "heal the sick, cleanse the lepers, raise the dead, cast out demons" (Matthew 10:8). Such works of God testified that God was present and that His Kingdom had come. Paul believed (as we should) that New Testament faith, powerful faith, is never in human wisdom but solely in the power of God.

History is replete with examples of those who lived by the power of God. While living in Great Britain, my wife and daughter and I decided to do that very European thing of taking the Eurail across Europe. One of our stops along the way was Prague in the Czech Republic. The city was of interest to me because of a reformer from that area by the name of Jan Hus.

Hus was a Catholic priest in the fourteenth century. During an era of power struggles and numerous questionable practices among church leadership, he was a strong preacher of the Word of God who understood and proclaimed the message of the Kingdom. Hus's message was not well received by the church of Rome. After a number of conflicts, they summoned him to the Council of Constance in Germany and condemned him to death. While his death was a tragedy, it led to a movement that eventually became the Moravian Church, one of the oldest Protestant denominations in the world. Claiming Hus as their spiritual patriarch, the Moravians sent hundreds of missionaries all over the world to preach the Gospel, becoming a powerful force for the Kingdom. Some Moravians even sold themselves into slavery in order to minister to slaves in the West Indies. The Moravians were no strangers to God's mighty power, as attested by a Dr. Greenfield in August 1727:

We saw the hand of God and His wonders, and we were all under the cloud of our fathers baptized with their Spirit. The Holy Ghost came upon us and in those days great signs and wonders took place in our midst. From that time scarcely a day passed but what we beheld His almighty workings amongst us.[4]

In Prague, as I faced the Jan Hus memorial in the old town square, I began to imagine what it must have been like five hundred years before. What was going through the minds of the people? I turned to some of the locals and asked them to tell me about Jan Hus. To my surprise, no one knew his story. His impact is now relegated to the history books. This is one reason why every generation needs a fresh move of God.

Eyewitnesses of Hope

It is hard to know exactly what to expect when starting a new church, but we hoped and prayed that Influence Church would be a place where God would do exactly what His Word promised. We lived every day with a sense of expectation. Little did we know that we would see countless miracles, the first of which took place within the first two months of the church's existence.

Skye, a 26-year-old mother of three children, was diagnosed with a brain tumor the circumference of a grapefruit. I felt, as did all who gathered around Skye to pray, that this was not how life should be. This was not a cleverly designed plot of the Father to strengthen her faith or to punish His children. Sickness was contrary to the way the Kingdom was supposed to work. It was our job to release all the promises of God on earth. Only then would the world understand that God is good.

It was during this time that I began to truly understand the goodness of the Father and the power of hope. I will let Skye tell her own story:

I asked God, "Please make me a miracle. Lord, I have three babies and one with special needs; they need me." The next Sunday at Influence, I met with Pastor Phil, Tammy and many other amazing people who prayed over me. I felt something supernatural happen that day. The next week I met with the neurosurgeon to discuss the results of my latest MRI. The doctor walked in and said very nonchalantly, "Well, the tumor is barely visible." He had no explanation why the tumor had shrunk to being "barely visible"! But I do. God can do anything through *faith*.

Four years later, Tammy was interviewing little Gracie, an eight-year-old who had prayed for a family friend. Gracie's friend Honey had been suffering from lung cancer and was told that she had only a short time to live. When Gracie heard that distressing news, she ran to Honey, put her arms around her and said, "You will live; you will not die, in Jesus' name." Two weeks later the doctors told Honey that the cancer was gone. When Gracie's mother asked her if she had heard about Honey, Gracie said, "She's healed, right?" Her mom asked how she knew. Her answer was, "Because I prayed for her to be healed."

Skye was living in Colorado Springs at the time, but she was at Influence that Sunday with her three children while on a visit with her parents. When Skye heard Gracie's story, she asked if we would pray for her seven-year-old son, Kruse, who has Down syndrome and had never spoken. He was also hitting himself on a daily basis to the point of drawing blood. A small group of people gathered around Kruse to pray.

The next day Skye sent me a text:

Yep, it's me! And I'm reporting another miracle. Kruse has been a different child. It's a true miracle from God! He was hitting himself every minute of the day, but he has not hit himself for two days.

And for the first time he spoke and said, "Mama," "Dada" and "Papa." This is *no* coincidence. God is so good.

After Kruse returned to school in Colorado Springs, his teacher called Skye to ask what had happened in California. "Kruse seems different," she reported, "and he is not hitting himself at school."

Skye was just one of many in our young church who could proclaim how God was at work, providing hope for all who attended. Katie was a young woman diagnosed with ovarian cancer weeks before her wedding. Her cancer was a physical threat to her life, of course, but it also took a toll on her emotional state because of her desire to have children. Three biopsies had confirmed the presence of cancer, so the doctor scheduled an operation to try to remove the tumor.

Before her surgery, we gathered around her for prayer. Her name was placed on the prayer wall (which I describe below), and we believed God for a miracle. That miracle took place before her surgery: After two and a half hours in the operating room, the surgeon emerged, her eyes swelling with tears and a huge smile on her face. "I don't know how, but the cancer is gone. Katie is going to be just fine." Not long afterward, Katie was in the hospital again—this time to deliver Mila, a beautiful daughter, demonstrating further proof of God's healing and mercy. Katie and Carlos have recently had a second child, and Katie enjoys good health and continued joy from the Lord. And we are continually reminded that God did not tell us to pray for the sick but rather to "heal the sick" (Matthew 10:8).

Twenty-five-year-old Ashley was another member during our church's first year who shared her story with me:

On September 26, 2012, my bladder stopped functioning. My urethra closed up completely, making it impossible to do one of the most natural voluntary bodily actions. After surgery number ten, I was ready to give up! It was then that members of the Influence prayer team prayed, asking God to rid me of all the physical and emotional pain from my past and present. God answered my prayers. He heard my cry!

The doctor confirmed my faith—he looked at me with confusion and a smile. He shook my hand and said, "I don't know how you did it, but you did. Let's go take the tube out. Congratulations!" I immediately covered my face and cried. Overwhelmed with happiness, I said out loud, *"Thank You, Jesus!"*

And then there was Faith. Faith was just three-and-a-half years old when she was diagnosed with a malignant skin cancer on her scalp. Her parents recalled,

Our first response was to have Pastor Phil and Tammy and the Influence prayer team pray for her complete healing. On July 2, 2014, we received a call from the doctor saying all signs of the cancer were gone! This is yet another testimony that Jesus still heals people. If you have a need that only God can answer, I encourage you to connect with the prayer ministry of Influence Church.

The location of Influence Church is unique: We meet in a former post office that we purchased from the United States Postal Service. Little did we know at the time that this purchase would be key to making a "house of prayer" for all people (Matthew 21:13).

When a visitor enters our lobby, the first thing he or she notices is the large wall of stones that fills the west side of the space. This is our prayer wall, which is filled with thousands of prayer requests wedged between the stones. Dozens of people each day enter our doors expecting to find the post office. Instead, they are greeted by a trained prayer warrior, who invites them to add their prayers to the wall.

On one occasion two Muslim women came in. When they were invited to add a prayer request to the wall, one of them began to cry, explaining that her sixteen-year-old son had a brain tumor and his prognosis was not good. She placed her request in the wall and then returned with her friend in a few days to add another request. Two weeks after that, they came back and gave our prayer team member a report of praise and thanksgiving. A visit to the doctor and additional tests revealed that her son's tumor was gone. They gave praise to Jesus and the miracle of the prayer wall. They explained that, as Muslims, they could not attend our services, but we assured them that they were always welcome to pray here and experience the miracle power of Jesus.

We firmly believe that the works of God reveal the heart of God and will draw people to true faith in God. We believe that, in some way, the presence of God has settled on our prayer wall. It is a touchpoint of faith and a symbol of the miraculous. The moment people enter our building, they sense that God is in our midst.

We have witnessed an acceleration of miracles at Influence as we gain a better understanding of the language of faith. Miracles seem to beget miracles. Miracles are waiting to be released as God makes His presence known on earth as it is in heaven.

I am convinced that when we live with a spirit of expectation, God meets that expectation. The absence of miracles today is not due to reluctance on God's part but rather a lack of understanding of how God works and a lack of prayer.

What God has done at Influence has been a miracle in and of itself. But beyond that, it seems to me, we are attempting to live out His revealed strategy for the end-time Church, one that reveals the goodness of the Father to an increasingly dark and lawless world.

Moving Forward with Hope

I have been thinking about this book for a long time, but I only set out to put it down in final form a few months ago. During that time, my country endured its worst mass shooting in history (Orlando, June 12, 2016) as well as the deadliest attack on law enforcement officers (Dallas, July 7, 2016). These and other national tragedies were exclamation points on the severity of the problem of lawlessness that weighed on my mind. The sad fact of the matter is that by the time this book is published, those statistics may already be outdated. The assurance of tomorrow for any of us is never certain.

But then, that has been true for centuries. From the onset of Christianity in the first century, those committed to truth have been persecuted by powers and people of darkness. Yet the Church has continued to grow and flourish, thanks to the never-failing power of God. As long as our hope is in God, we will never succumb to the influence of the darkness (Romans 5:1–5).

Many people think *hope* is an iffy, fingers-crossed, uncertain sensation. ("I hope it doesn't rain on our picnic today." "I hope we're able to pay the bills this month." "I hope God is big enough to handle our latest crisis.") But Christian hope is very different. Believers have hope because Jesus Himself is present and actively involved in their lives. Christ *is* our hope (Colossians 1:27). There is nothing iffy or uncertain about that. No matter how bad the situation appears to get, and regardless of the power of lawlessness that besets us, we can have confidence that we will ultimately overcome it with the power of God.

Jesus' disciples noticed that prayer was essential to His power, which fired their desire to learn how to pray (Luke 11:1). In response He gave them what we know as the Lord's Prayer (Matthew 6:9–13), in which we are taught to pray, "Your kingdom come. Your will be done on earth as it is in heaven." *On earth as it is in heaven*. What a powerful idea—we can release heaven on earth through prayer. This is a key to changing society and preventing the spread of evil. We are to "bind the strong man" (demonic spirit) and release God's Kingdom on earth (Matthew 12:29). When we do this, we will begin to see a new wave of power, healing, joy and hope in the Holy Spirit.

When we honor Jesus as Lord and submit to His authority, we put the darkness on notice that we are serious about the Kingdom of God. Then the God-given dominion that is rightfully ours is reestablished and the Spirit is free to move. Jesus' Kingdom and power are a present reality. We live under an open heaven where all of its resources are at our disposal.

As we pray and seek righteousness, we destroy the works of the evil one. The only hope for holding back the spread of lawlessness is God's presence, which overwhelms the spread of evil in our lands. Think about God's willingness to heed the prayer of Abraham to spare the city of Sodom (Genesis 18:22–33). Abraham knew the heart of God; he knew that God was compassionate and full of mercy. He also knew that prayer would move the heart of God. When he asked God to spare the city if fifty righteous people could be found in it, God agreed. And then Abraham kept asking for more. How about forty-five righteous people? Forty? Thirty? Twenty? God agreed to each new request, as well as Abraham's final one: He would spare the city if there were just ten righteous people in it. We who live in these days of increased wickedness need to pay close attention to this account and see how the power of prayer can move God.

In many current discussions about the end times, the "message beneath the message" seems to be an attempt to either entertain or terrify people. But the Bible's forewarning about increasing lawlessness was never meant to drive us into a panic. Paul assured us, "God did not appoint us to wrath, but to obtain salvation through our Lord Jesus Christ, who died for us . . . Therefore comfort each other and edify one another, just as you also are doing" (1 Thessalonians 5:9, 11).

We are living in a unique day of the fullness of the Spirit and the fullness of time. Jesus revealed to the disciples that His words and power inaugurated a new day unlike any other. It was an announcement of power and revelation. His promise to them (and to future generations) is exciting: "For I tell you that many prophets and kings have desired to see what you see, and have not seen it, and to hear what you hear, and have not heard it" (Luke 10:24).

It is my prayer that this book leaves you with a sense of renewed confidence and hope in our wise, powerful and gracious God. His perpetual presence, and your access to Him through prayer, will enable you to anticipate struggles, make wise decisions and avoid tendencies to panic when you hear frightening news. Although the world may continue to increase in lawlessness, fear and conflict, we can move forward in the power of God, bind the strong man and see the miraculous outpouring of the Spirit of God.

Notes

Chapter 1: The Problem of Lawlessness

1. The complete account of the Israelites before the mountain is found in Exodus 19.

2. Suzanne Russell, "Witness: Rabbi Runs into Burning Synagogue to Save Torah," *USA Today*, October 23, 2015, http://www.usatoday.com/story/news/nation-now/2015/10/23/fire-engulfs-historic-new-jersey-synagogue/74488174/.

3. Joseph Shapiro, "Amish Forgive School Shooter, Struggle with Grief," *National Public Radio*, October 2, 2007, http://www.npr.org/templates/story/story.php?storyId=14900930.

Chapter 2: The Evil in All of Us

1. David Cesarani, "Adolf Eichmann: The Mind of a War Criminal," *BBC History*, February 17, 2011, http://www.bbc.co.uk/history/worldwars/genocide/eichmann_01.shtml.

2. "Vienna: Historical Background," Yad Vashem World Holocaust Remembrance Center, accessed November 2, 2016, http://www.yadvashem.org/yv/en/righteous/stories/historical_background/vienna.asp.

3. Richard J. Evans, review of *Eichmann before Jerusalem: The Unexamined Life of a Mass Murderer*, by Bettina Stangneth, *Guardian US*, October 17, 2014,

https://www.theguardian.com/books/2014/oct/17/eichmann-before-jerusalem
-bettina-stangneth-review.

4. "Adolf Eichmann," United States Holocaust Memorial Museum, accessed November 2, 2016, https://www.ushmm.org/wlc/en/article.php?ModuleId =10007412.

5. Charles Colson, *The Body: Being Light in Darkness* (Dallas: Word Publishing, 1992), 181–182. See also *60 Minutes*, vol. 15, no. 21, aired February 6, 1983.

6. John F. Walvoord and Roy B. Zuck, eds., *Bible Knowledge Commentary: Old Testament*, (Colorado Springs: Cook Communications Ministries, 1983), under "Ezekiel: Judgment on Gentile Nations: Judgment on Tyre."

7. Art Lindsley, "The Problem of Evil: C. S. Lewis Speaks to Life's Most Difficult Questions," *Knowing & Doing*, Winter 2003, http://www.cslewisinstitute .org/webfm_send/636.

8. Ibid.

9. Robert Gittings, ed., *John Keats: Selected Letters* (New York: Oxford University Press, 2002), 232.

10. C. S. Lewis, *The Problem of Pain* (New York: HarperOne, 1996), 65.

11. For an informative and detailed explanation of moving through the levels of developmental psychology, see Keith M. Eigel and Karl W. Kuhnert, *The Map* (Friendswood, Tex.: Baxter Press, 2016).

Chapter 3: Lawlessness in America: A Case Study

1. James D. Horan and Paul Sann, *Pictorial History of the Wild West* (New York: Bonanza Books, 1954), 10.

2. Ibid., 9.

3. James P. Owen, *Cowboy Ethics: What Wall Street Can Learn from the Code of the West* (Ketchum, Idaho: Stoecklein Publishing, 2004), 24.

4. Ibid., 45.

5. William H. Forbis, *The Cowboys*, vol. 1 of *The Old West* (New York: Time-Life Books, 1973), 210.

6. "Trail of Tears," History.com, accessed August 15, 2016, http://www.history.com/topics/native-american-history/trail-of-tears.

7. "The War to End All Wars," *BBC News*, November 10, 1998, http://news .bbc.co.uk/2/hi/special_report/1998/10/98/world_war_i/198172.stm.

8. Paul Sann, *The Lawless Decade* (Mineola, N.Y.: Dover Publications, 1957, 2010), 9.

9. "The Weather Underground: The Movement," *Independent Lens*, accessed November 2, 2016, http://www.pbs.org/independentlens/weatherunderground /movement.html.

10. Aleksandr Solzhenitsyn, *Warning to the West* (New York: Farrar, Straus and Giroux, 1976), 79.

11. American Safety Council, "Aggressive Driving and Road Rage," accessed August 30, 2016, http://www.safemotorist.com/articles/road_rage.aspx.

12. Bonnie Berkowitz, Lazaro Gamio, Denise Lu, Kevin Uhrmacher, and Todd Lindeman, "The Math of Mass Shootings," *Washington Post*, July 27, 2016, https:// www.washingtonpost.com/graphics/national/mass-shootings-in-america/. The definition of *mass shooting* can vary, but the *Post* defined it as an event in which four or more people are killed by a lone shooter or, in rare cases, two shooters. Their totals do not include gang killings, shootings that result from robberies or other crimes or deaths that involve only the family members of the shooter.

Chapter 4: The Men of Nineveh

1. Darrell L. Bock, *A Theology of Luke and Acts* (Grand Rapids: Zondervan, 2012), 400.

2. Merrill C. Tenney, ed., *The Zondervan Pictorial Bible Dictionary* (Grand Rapids: Zondervan, 1967), 588.

3. Marc Van De Mieroop, *A History of the Ancient Near East, ca. 3000–323 BC* (Oxford: Blackwell Publishing, 2004), 218.

4. Karen Radner, *Ancient Assyria: A Very Short Introduction* (Oxford: Oxford University Press, 2015), 6.

5. As a point of interest, one of Nahum's statements has elicited much discussion among students of prophecy. In describing the glory of Nineveh (that would soon be coming to an end), he wrote, "The chariots rage in the streets, they jostle one another in the broad roads; they seem like torches, they run like lightning" (Nahum 2:4). Does it sound as if Nahum might have been envisioning the coming of automobile traffic? Some people have believed so, and perhaps they are right. While it is an interesting speculation, it was never a generally accepted interpretation. Still, Nahum's observation shows that ancient Nineveh must have been quite an impressive place.

6. Jessica Lewis McFate and Christopher Kozak, "America Is Acting Locally, the Islamic State Is Thinking Globally," *Foreign Policy*, July 11, 2016, http: //foreignpolicy.com/2016/07/11/america-is-acting-locally-the-islamic-state -is-thinking-globally/.

7. "Ancient Nineveh: Ancient Manners and Customs, Daily Life, Cultures, and Bible Lands," Bible Study Online, accessed November 13, 2016, http://www.bible-history.com/biblestudy/nineveh.html.

8. Simon Anglim, Phyllis G. Jestice, Rob S. Rice, Scott M. Rusch, and John Serrati, *Fighting Techniques of the Ancient World: 3000 B.C.—A.D. 500* (London: Amber Books, 2002), 185.

9. Sam Greenhill, Jill Reilly, and Kieran Corcoran, "ISIS Butchers Leave 'Roads Lined with Decapitated Police and Soldiers': Battle for Baghdad Looms as Thousands Answer Iraqi Government's Call to Arms and Jihadists Bear Down on Capital," *Daily Mail*, June 12, 2014, www.dailymail.co.uk/news/article-2655977/ISIS-militants-march-Baghdad-trademark-bullet-head-gets-way-control-north.html.

10. Jennifer Newton, "ISIS Burn 19 Yazidi Girls to Death in Iron Cages after They Refused to Have Sex with Jihadists," *Daily Mail*, June 6, 2016, www.dailymail.co.uk/news/article-3627063/ISIS-burn-19-Yazidi-girls-death-iron-cages-refused-sex-jihadists.html.

11. Michael McCaul, chairman, "Worldwide Threats to the Homeland: ISIS and the New Wave of Terror," opening statement of the hearing before the House Homeland Security Committee, 114th Cong., July 14, 2016, https://homeland.house.gov/wp-content/uploads/2016/07/07-14-16-McCaul-Open-1.pdf.

12. Radner, *Ancient Assyria*, 11.

13. Erika Belibtreu, "Grisly Assyrian Record of Torture and Death," *Biblical Archaeology Review* 17, no. 1 (January/February 1991), http://faculty.uml.edu/ethan_Spanier/Teaching/documents/CP6.0AssyrianTorture.pdf.

14. Holly Yan and Nadeem Muaddi, "Why the Battle for Mosul Matters in the Fight against ISIS," CNN, October 17, 2016, http://www.cnn.com/2016/10/17/middleeast/battle-for-mosul/index.html.

15. Radner, *Ancient Assyria*, 16.

16. Yan and Muaddi, "Battle for Mosul."

17. Andrew Curry, "Here Are the Ancient Sites ISIS Has Damaged and Destroyed," *National Geographic*, September 1, 2015, http://news.nationalgeographic.com/2015/09/150901-isis-destruction-looting-ancient-sites-iraq-syria-archaeology/.

18. The internet can sometimes be curiously insightful. A quick Google search on "men of Nineveh" yielded the expected illustrations of ancient art and architecture and portrayals of Jonah. But among them were a number of images I had not anticipated: recent photos of cloaked, sword-wielding ISIS members!

19. P. W. Singer and Emerson Brooking, "Terror on Twitter: How ISIS Is Taking War to Social Media—and How Social Media Is Fighting Back," *Popular Science*, December 11, 2015, www.popsci.com/terror-on-twitter-how-isis-is-taking-war-to-social-media.

20. President George W. Bush, address to the CENTCOM Coalition Conference, Tampa, Florida, May 1, 2007, http://georgewbush-whitehouse.archives.gov/news/releases/2007/05/text/20070501-4.html.

21. R. Edward Miller, *Secrets of the Argentine Revival* (Peachtree City, Ga.: Peniel Outreach Ministries, 1999), 18.

22. "The Argentine Revival of 1954," America Pray Now, March 2, 2015, http://americapraynow.com/Revivals/the-argentine-revival-of-1954.html.

23. Joel C. Rosenberg, "Study Finds 10 Million Muslims Have Become Followers of Christ Since 1960," *Joel C. Rosenberg's Blog*, May 27, 2016, https://flashtrafficblog.wordpress.com/2016/05/27/study-finds-10-million-muslims-have-become-followers-of-christ-since-1960/.

24. Joel C. Rosenberg, *Epicenter: Why the Current Rumblings in the Middle East Will Change Your Future* (Carol Stream, Ill.: Tyndale, 2006, 2008), 203–223.

Chapter 5: The Rise of Israel

1. Norman Grubb, *C. T. Studd, Cricketer and Pioneer* (Fort Washington, Pa.: CLC Publications, 1933), 162.

2. Albert Hourani, *A History of the Arab Peoples* (Cambridge, Mass.: Belknap Press, 1991), 16.

3. Witton T. Davies, "Islam: A Sketch with Bibliography," *The Biblical World* 8, no. 5 (1896): 338.

4. Bill Johnson, *Experience the Impossible* (Bloomington, Minn.: Chosen, 2014), 51.

5. Megan Garber, "How Many Stars Are There in the Sky?" *The Atlantic*, November 19, 2013, http://www.theatlantic.com/technology/archive/2013/11/how-many-stars-are-there-in-the-sky/281641/. Only about 2,500 stars are visible to the naked eye at any one time.

6. Mark Twain, "Concerning the Jews," *Harper's Magazine*, September 1899, quoted in the Modern History Sourcebook, Fordham University, accessed November 15, 2016, http://sourcebooks.fordham.edu/mod/1898twain-jews.asp.

7. Wayne Grudem, *Systematic Theology: An Introduction to Biblical Doctrine* (Grand Rapids: Zondervan, 1994), 337.

8. Joseph Farah, "An Unconventional Arab Viewpoint," WND, February 24, 2003, http://www.wnd.com/2003/02/17425/.

9. F. E. Peters, *Jerusalem: The Holy City in the Eyes of Chroniclers, Visitors, Pilgrims, and Prophets from the Days of Abraham to the Beginnings of Modern Times* (Princeton: Princeton University Press, 1985), 411.

10. Rabbi Alexander Davis, "Napoleon and the Jews," Beth El Synagogue, July 29, 2014, http://www.bethelsynagogue.org/napoleon-and-the-jews/.

11. Samuel B. Huntington, *The Clash of Civilizations* (New York: Touchstone, 1996), 94.

12. Efraim Karsh, *Islamic Imperialism* (New Haven, Conn.: Yale University Press, 2007), 1.

13. John Adams, letter to the Massachusetts Militia, October 11, 1798, http://founders.archives.gov/documents/Adams/99-02-02-3102.

14. Christopher Buck, *Religious Myths and Visions of America: How Minority Faiths Redefined America's World Role* (Westport, Conn.: Praeger Publishers, 2009), 136.

15. David Bosworth, *The Millennium and Related Events* (Chicago: Revell, 1889).

Chapter 6: Strange Alliances and Shaken Nations

1. Campbell Robertson, "Iraq Suffers as the Euphrates River Dwindles," *New York Times*, July 13, 2009.

2. "Red China: Firecracker No. 2," *Time* 85, no. 21 (1965): 35.

3. Israel Ministry of Foreign Affairs, "Law of Return 5710–1950," July 5, 1950, http://www.mfa.gov.il/mfa/mfa-archive/1950-1959/pages/law%20of%20return%205710-1950.aspx.

4. Joel Brinkley, "Ethiopian Jews and Israelis Exult as Airlift Is Completed," *New York Times*, May 26, 1991, http://www.nytimes.com/1991/05/26/world/ethiopian-jews-and-israelis-exult-as-airlift-is-completed.html.

5. Michael Lipka, "The Continuing Decline of Europe's Jewish Population," The Pew Research Center, February 9, 2015, http://www.pewresearch.org/fact-tank/2015/02/09/europes-jewish-population/.

6. "European and Foreign Country Population Data," JewishGen, accessed December 16, 2016, http://www.jewishgen.org/databases/GivenNames/dbdespop.htm.

7. Benjamin Netanyahu, address at Auschwitz concentration camp, Oswiecim, Poland, January 27, 2010, http://www.mfa.gov.il/mfa/pressroom/2010/pages/address_pm_netanyahu_at_auschwitz_27-jan-2010.aspx.

8. "Ancient Kush or 'Ethiopia,'" Ta Neter Foundation, accessed December 16, 2016, http://www.taneter.org/ethiopia.html.

9. Merrill Tenney, ed., *The Zondervan Pictorial Encyclopedia of the Bible*, vol. 1: A–C (Grand Rapids: Zondervan, 1975), s.v. "Cush."

10. Martin W. Lewis, "The Migration of Place Names: Africa, Libya, Ethiopia, Eritrea, and Sudan," GeoCurrents, December 5, 2011, http://www.geocurrents.info/historical-geography/the-migration-of-place-names-africa-libya-ethiopia-eritrea-and-sudan#ixzz4SMtK89nS.

11. G. W. Bromiley, ed., *The New International Standard Bible Encyclopedia, Volume Three: K–P* (Grand Rapids: Eerdmans, 1986), 222.

12. William Smith, *Smith's Bible Dictionary* (Nashville: Thomas Nelson, 2004), 416.

13. Arno C. Gaebelein, *The Prophet Ezekiel: An Analytical Exposition* (Neptune, N.J.: Loizeaux Brothers, 1918), 258.

14. Ehsan Yarshater, "Communication," *Iranian Studies* 22, no. 1 (1989): 62.

15. John Hagee, *Jerusalem Countdown* (Lake Mary, Fla.: FrontLine, 2006), 106.

16. Charles Lee Feinberg, *The Prophecy of Ezekiel* (Chicago: Moody, 1969), 221.

17. Caroline Copley, "Germany to Tell People to Stockpile Food and Water in Case of Attacks: FAS," *Reuters*, August 21, 2016, http://www.reuters.com/article/us-germany-security-stockpiling-idUSKCN10W0MJ.

18. "Turkey: Military Strength," Global Firepower, accessed November 18, 2016, http://www.globalfirepower.com/country-military-strength-detail.asp?country_id=turkey.

19. Darrell G. Young, "Iran in Bible Prophecy: The Prince of Persia," Focus on Jerusalem Prophecy Ministry, October 2004, http://focusonjerusalem.com/iraninbibleprophecy.html.

20. Brenda Shaffer, *Partners in Need: The Strategic Relationship of Russia and Iran*, Policy Paper no. 57 (Washington, D.C.: Washington Institute for Near East Policy, 2001), xi, http://www.washingtoninstitute.org/policy-analysis/view/partners-in-need-the-strategic-relationship-of-russia-and-iran.

21. Louis Charbonneau, "Update 6—In New York, Defiant Ahmadinejad Says Israel Will Be 'Eliminated,'" *Reuters*, September 24, 2012, http://www.reuters.com/article/un-assembly-ahmadinejad-idUSL1E8KO5BL20120924.

22. Harriet Mallinson, "Turkey Warns It Could LEAVE NATO because of a 'Lack of Support by the West' as the Country Forms Close Ties with Russia,"

Daily Mail, August 10, 2016, http://www.dailymail.co.uk/news/article-3733654/Turkey-warns-LEAVE-NATO-lack-support-West-country-forms-close-ties-Russia.html.

23. Samuel P. Huntington, *The Clash of Civilizations and the Remaking of World Order* (New York: Touchstone, 1996), 110.

24. Robert W. Merry, "The West and Islam," *Washington Times*, November 16, 2015, http://www.washingtontimes.com/news/2015/nov/16/robert-merry-clash-between-west-and-islam/.

Chapter 7: The Antichrist: Man of Lawlessness

1. Blaise Pascal, *Pensées* (New York: Penguin Classics, 1966, 1995), 45.

2. For a more thorough explanation of the justification and implementation of martial law as provided in the Constitution, see Steve Mount, "Constitutional Topic: Martial Law," U.S. Constitution Online, accessed December 9, 2016, http://www.usconstitution.net/consttop_mlaw.html.

3. Peter Schiff, "Let's Start a Third World War to Save the Global Economy," *Business Insider*, July 20, 2010, http://www.businessinsider.com/lets-pretend-to-have-another-second-world-war-to-boost-the-economy-2010-7.

4. Joy Allmond, "Is New York City on the Brink of a Great Awakening?" Christianity.com, November 19, 2013, http://www.christianity.com/christian-life/is-new-york-city-on-the-brink-of-a-great-awakening.html.

5. John Miller, interview with Osama bin Laden, *Frontline*, May 1998, http://www.pbs.org/wgbh/pages/frontline/shows/binladen/who/interview.html.

6. The Religion of Peace, accessed August 29, 2016, https://www.thereligionofpeace.com. For an explanation of the methodology used to maintain the list, including the quote in the text, see https://www.thereligionofpeace.com/pages/site/the-list.aspx.

Chapter 8: Spiritual Warfare

1. Col. Edward T. Imparato, USAF (ret.), *General MacArthur Wisdom and Visions* (Nashville: Turner Publishing, 2000), iBooks edition, 267.

2. Martin Luther King Jr., "Rediscovering Lost Values" (sermon, Second Baptist Church, Detroit, Mich., February 28, 1954), http://okra.stanford.edu/transcription/document_images/Vol02Scans/248_28-Feb-1954_Rediscovering%20Lost%20Values.pdf.

3. Aleksandr Solzhenitsyn, *The Gulag Archipelago*, abr. (New York: Harper Perennial Modern Classics, 2007), 79.

4. Ibid., xxii.

5. "Famous Women in Hungarian History," Consulate General of Hungary, New York, accessed November 29, 2016, http://consulate.newyork.gov.hu/famous-women-in-hungarian-history.

6. "Ilona Tóth, the Hungarian Jeanne d'Arc," HungarianAmbiance.com, November 7, 2009, http://www.hungarianambiance.com/2009/11/ilona-toth-hungarian-jeanne-darc.html.

7. "1900 Figures Forecast a Century's Dangers," ABC News, accessed November 28, 2016, http://abcnews.go.com/US/story?id=89965&page=1.

8. Bill Johnson, *When Heaven Invades Earth* (Shippensburg, Pa.: Treasure House, 2003), 64.

9. Charles R. Parsons, *An Hour With George Müller, The Man of Faith to Whom God Gave Millions* (Whitefish, Mont.: Literary Licensing, 2011), 10.

10. Miller, *Argentine Revival*, 64.

11. Miller, *Argentine Revival*, 18.

Chapter 9: How God Deals with Evil

1. United States v. George Wilson, 32 U.S. 150 (1833); see also "United States v. George Wilson," Legal Information Institute, accessed November 30, 2016, https://www.law.cornell.edu/supremecourt/text/32/150.

2. Norman L. Geisler, *If God, Why Evil?* (Minneapolis: Bethany House, 2011), 10.

3. Michael J. Sandel, *Justice* (New York: Farrar, Straus and Giroux, 2009), 9.

4. John Eadie, *Commentary on the Epistle to the Ephesians* (Grand Rapids: Zondervan, 1977), 473.

5. Miroslav Volf, *Exclusion and Embrace* (Nashville: Abingdon, 1996), 303.

6. Kim Sue Lia Perkes, "Religion Is Drug-War Weapon, Official Says," *Arizona Republic*, June 12, 1990.

7. Volf, *Exclusion*, 304.

8. Paul Billheimer, *Destined for the Throne* (Minneapolis: Bethany House, 1996), 53.

9. Ravi Zacharias, *Deliver Us from Evil* (Nashville: W Publishing Group, 1997), 172.

10. Mike Bickle and Brian Kim, *7 Commitments for Spiritual Growth* (Kansas City: Forerunner Publishing, 2009, 2015), iBooks edition, 25.

11. Elisabeth Elliott, *A Chance to Die* (Grand Rapids: Revell, 2005), 85.

12. Dietrich Bonhoeffer, *Letters and Papers from Prison* (New York: Touchstone, 1997), 5.

13. Reinhard Bonnke, *Time Is Running Out* (Orlando: E-R Productions, 2008), iBooks edition, 166.

14. Lewis, *Problem of Pain*, 172.

15. Bill Johnson, *Face to Face with God* (Lake Mary, Fla.: Charisma House, 2007), 215.

Chapter 10: Looking Forward with Hope

1. A. W. Tozer, *The Knowledge of the Holy* (San Francisco: Harper & Row, 1961), 89.

2. Billheimer, *Destined*, 45.

3. E. M. Bounds, *E. M. Bounds on Prayer* (Peabody, Mass.: Hendrickson Publishers, 2006), 172.

4. Jerry Lesac, *Crop Circles and Climate Change* (Maitland, Fla.: Xulon Press, 2008), 149.

Index

Phil Hotsenpiller is an entrepreneur, author and cultural thought leader. Throughout his career, he has worked extensively on issues at the nexus of leadership, artistry and contemporary culture.

Phil earned his B.A. and M.Div., going on to conduct postgraduate studies at Oxford University. He and his wife, Tammy, founded Influence Church in Anaheim Hills, California.

Phil is the founder and president of New York Executive Coaching Group, a firm that has assisted presidents, CEOs and other professionals to achieve breakthrough results in their professional and personal lives. His clients are a diverse and accomplished array of leaders from Fortune 500 companies, the arts and entertainment, finance, industry and not-for-profit programs.

Phil's passion is for teaching and ministering the Word of God. He is considered an authority on end-time prophecy and has been interviewed by *The Washington Post, USA Today,* CNN, *The Christian Post,* The History Channel and *The Telegraph* on the subject of Armageddon and the post-apocalyptic world. Phil also conducts regular interviews with various media outlets, including Fox News Channel.

Phil is a co-author of the eight-book series Passionate Lives and Leaders, in which real-world leaders share their experiences in building passionate teams and organizations. This series is a guide to harnessing the passion that leads to outstanding performance and gaining the competitive edge, and it explores the four underlying facts that are necessary for a business to achieve pure performance and success.

In all of his personal and professional endeavors, Phil is committed to fostering creativity, challenging leaders, developing conversations across diverse communities and advancing the Kingdom of God.